POLARITIES
OF MAN'S EXISTENCE
IN BIBLICAL PERSPECTIVE

POLARITIES
OF
MAN'S
EXISTENCE
IN
BIBLICAL
PERSPECTIVE

by Frank Stagg

THE WESTMINSTER PRESS
PHILADELPHIA

PUBLISHED BY THE WESTMINSTER PRESS®

PHILADELPHIA, PENNSYLVANIA

PRINTED IN THE UNITED STATES OF AMERICA

Library of Congress Cataloging in Publication Data

Stagg, Frank, 1911–
    Polarities of man's existence in Biblical
perspective.

    Bibliography : p.
    1. Man (Theology)   I. Title.
BT701.2.S68   233   73–8812
ISBN 0–664–20976–9

To
the memory of
John Baillie
who at many points,
to borrow his own way of putting it,
"helped me clarify my own thinking"

CONTENTS

FOREWORD

This book was conceived in my mind nearly ten years ago, and it seemed to be in the delivery room some years ago. Then "the floods descended": an avalanche of editorial and writing assignments; a five-year term as managing editor of *Review and Expositor,* theological journal of the faculty of the Southern Baptist Theological Seminary; and almost simultaneously an appointment as a consulting editor for the New Testament division of *Broadman Bible Commentary,* with writing assignments for the commentaries on Matthew and Philippians. This book went into cold storage until relief came about two years ago.

Although this is intended to be a doctrine of man from Biblical perspective, it is not intended to be a comprehensive review of Biblical material on man. Rather, as the title indicates, it is concerned primarily with man in certain polar situations, where he is claimed from two sides at once and where he finds his authentic existence in the resulting tension.

Whatever expertise I have is in the Biblical field, in particular in the Greek New Testament. The reader will soon see that I interact not only with Scripture but also with competing views. Biblical writers themselves interacted, consciously or not, with cultural "trajectories" (thrusts) that to some extent drew proponents and opponents into their wake (cf. James M. Robinson and Helmut Koester, *Trajectories Through Early Christianity;*

Fortress Press, 1971). Since such study necessarily spills over into areas outside the range of my expertise, at some points heavy dependence is placed upon specialists in these areas. Major interaction is with the Greek New Testament, the author's almost daily companion for thirty-five years. Secondary sources are at a minimum there, although such sources have contributed heavily through the past decades.

Attention is given to relevance, with sufficient but, I hope, not excessive stress. I have no interest at all in playing in some "theological sandbox." Theology interests me only to the extent that it affects my existence as a person and as a servant of Christ. This very preoccupation with man reflects that interest.

One apprehension in submitting this book is that it may do less than justice to the Jews, to whom we owe the most and the best of our heritage. The book must necessarily take issue with certain views and values belonging to certain Jews in Biblical times. I will be grieved if this in any way reflects or encourages sectarian bias. The fact is that the study centers in a basically Jewish situation where often Jewish views are opposed to Jewish views, as is true in the Old Testament itself. Tensions run through all religious groups, including Jewish and Christian. Advance is made through give-and-take within each group. If at points we take issue with some Jewish thought, it basically is because we also are guided by Jewish thought, in both Testaments.

Special thanks are given to three of my colleagues who read certain chapters of the manuscript and gave me the benefit of their observations: Professors John D. W. Watts, Eric C. Rust, and Wayne E. Oates, who read Chapter 1, Chapters 2 and 4, and Chapter 5, respectively. Of course they are not responsible for limitations that yet remain in the book. Appreciated also are Miss Jean Aiken and her staff in the office services of the Southern Baptist Theological Seminary. As usual, my wife bore the burden of the first typing and afforded the invaluable service of reader reaction.

F. S.

Louisville, Kentucky

INTRODUCTION

Anthropology belongs properly to theology.[1] What is man? Who is man? What is his origin, nature, and destiny? What is his plight? What threatens him? What is it to be lost? What is it to be saved? What is required of man? What is his task? How is he related to God, to other persons, to the material order? It is proper to give man a primary place in theology, as he has in Scripture.

This is not to suggest that man put himself at the center of theology. It is "the inversion of faith" whenever man "puts himself into the center, constructs an anthropocentric universe, and makes confidence in his own value rather than faith in God his beginning." [2] But it is to be recognized that man cannot escape himself, even in theology. All theology is in a real sense man's understanding of that about which he theologizes, and this includes himself.

This by no means denies the revelation of God nor his initiative behind authentic theology. To me the initial Biblical claim is primary: "In the beginning God" (Gen. 1:1). I presuppose the initiative of God at every significant point: creation, revelation, redemption. Nonetheless, when theology has been formulated and proclaimed, it is through the mouth or pen of man. It is man's understanding of God, of himself, and of his situation. Revelation is the self-disclosure of God to man. It is revelation through something which happens, or which God causes to happen, an event that awakens faith and gives understanding and direction. To Christian faith, the culminating event is that in which the Word became flesh and dwelt among us (John 1:1, 14).

It is philosophy and not theology if man's understanding of existence is his alone. It is theology if it is an understanding reached in the presence of God and in interaction with God. Even so, man yet does not escape himself when he theologizes. He cannot step out of his own skin. He begins with himself, and however far beyond himself he may see, he yet sees from the perspective of man. A student's impatient protest to his professor, "Why don't you give us God's viewpoint?" was well-meaning but overlooked the simple fact that the professor is not God and strictly speaking cannot speak from "God's viewpoint." Man can "view" only from the "point" at which he stands.

There is here concurrence with the insight of Cocceius (1603–1669) : *Ho theologos est ho ton theon, ek tou theou, enōpion tou theou, eis doxan autou legōn* ("The theologian is the one saying 'God!' from God, in the presence of God, and unto his glory").[3] Truest theology is doxology. H. Richard Niebuhr well said, "We acknowledge revelation by no third person proposition, such as that there is a God, but only in the direct confession of the heart, 'Thou art my God.' " [4] Theology at its best is not talk about God but enjoyment of the presence of God and the praise of God, for God is "not an inference but a Presence." [5] Wayne Oates aptly says, "The excruciating theological necessity in men's lives today is not assent to the proposition of the existence of God but first-hand experience in communicating with him." [6] Although this book is about man, it is not forgotten that in every way the priority belongs to God.

Even though God is there from the beginning and even though it is his first speaking to us that awakens us and enables us, it yet remains true that man sees and hears and thinks out of his own existence as he responds to God, to other persons, and to the events about him. Man is admittedly conditioned by space, time, and his own finitude; and he cannot describe God as God is in himself but only as God encounters him. Neither can man know himself in any unconditioned way. What we hear and see is an act of faith, conditioned as we are; but this does not necessarily invalidate what we hear and see.[7]

This book is written in the faith that there were men of God who stood in the presence of great moments and events in history in which God disclosed himself to man and in which he made known his will and his way for man. It is written in the faith that there were men who, "borne along by the Holy Spirit, spoke from God" (II Peter 1:21).[8] It is written in the faith that "every God-breathed Scripture is also profitable for teaching, for re-proof, for correction, for instruction in righteousness, that the man of God may be equipped for every good work" (II Tim. 3: 16 f.). It sees the Old Testament as the prophetic witness to God's creative, revelatory, and redemptive work in the creation of his people. It sees the New Testament as preserving the apostolic witness to God's culminating work through the mighty event at the center of which is Jesus Christ. It sees continuity and ful-fillment, unity and variety, in these diverse writings which across many centuries took shape and found their way into one corpus.

Although God is not dead or retired but rather is alive and yet speaking to his people, this book is written out of a belief in the primacy and uniqueness of Scripture, in particular as the prophetic and apostolic witness to events unique in salvation history. This book does attempt to capture something of Biblical perspective as it bears upon the understanding of man, with special attention to man's "polar" situations.

The Biblical view of man contrasts sharply with various non-Biblical views, and to miss the Biblical view of man distorts al-most all else that concerns Biblical theology.[9] To go no farther, one cannot have a view of sin or salvation that is sounder than his view of man. To misunderstand man is to misunderstand his plight and his deliverance from that plight. This book will con-cern itself with man's nature and with his sin and his salvation.

By the "polarities of our existence" is meant the claims be-tween which we find our existence. These claims may seem to be contradictory or conflicting, yet it is only in a paradoxical sense that this is true. We necessarily live in certain tensions, finding our being between what appear to be opposite claims made upon us. The tensions with which we are concerned here are not tensions imposed upon us from without in the sense that outside pressures impinge upon us, but they represent something more fundamental. They are polar realities that belong necessarily to our existence. We live under tensions that belong inherently, necessarily, and properly to the life to which we are called.

What we are talking about is not "middle of the roadism." To take one's half in the middle of the road is both greedy and dangerous. As William A. Mueller put it in conversation, "One thus can get bumped from both sides." What we are talking about is not to be confused with "straddling the fence." That can be not only cowardly but ridiculous, and the alternative to straddling the fence need not be to come down on one side or the other. It may be to abolish the fence and draw the lines another way. What we have in mind by "polarities of our existence" is not compromise, although compromise itself may be good; compromise may be finding common ground with others. The "expediency" that sacrifices principle for selfish gain is to be spurned. But by "polarities" neither compromise nor expediency is implied.

What is meant here is the comprehensiveness in which we find our existence. To understand this is to see ourselves as created in the image of God, in the image of God but not God, and to see ourselves as creatures yet more than creatures. It is to see ourselves as highly complex yet holistic, as aspective yet not partitive. It is to see ourselves as individuals, with an individuality that belongs necessarily and permanently to personal existence, yet at the same time as corporate, unable to have our being alone. It is to see ourselves as made yet in the making, as *being* yet in need of *becoming*. It is to see ourselves as free yet bound, as subjects yet objects, as sinners yet saints, as called to deny self yet affirm self, as called to "hate" ourselves yet love ourselves, as called to a salvation that is absolutely free yet costing everything, as pure gift yet absolute demand.

In short, it is to see that the truth about our being and our existence is too big for simple statement. No one verbal net can capture it. It is a truth so big that it can be stated only in paradox, in seeming contradiction. But the "polarity" is more than semantic. The polar situations are real. We see ourselves finding our true existence between various "poles," drawn toward each but never to either pole to the exclusion of the other. It is tension indeed, but necessary creative tension.

Psalm 8 as adapted by the author of Hebrews (Heb. 2:5–13) will serve as the point of departure for the study. The basic question throughout will be "What is man?" There will follow no exhaustive study of Hebrews, although much of its message will be drawn upon, and effort will be made to draw heavily upon the whole Bible, especially the New Testament, in this attempt to see man from Biblical perspective.

What is man? Who is man? That is our inquiry. Is it enough to call him *homo sapiens,* the rational animal? *Homo faber,* the maker or doer? *Homo orans,* the worshiper or praying species? Is it enough to leave man to science to be classified biologically or zoologically? Can his humanity be understood in terms alone of his animality or his kinship to the divine? What is it to understand man as a human being, i.e., as being human? [10]

Chapter 1

CREATED
IN THE IMAGE OF GOD

In an adaptation of Ps. 8, the author of Hebrews (Heb. 2:5 ff.) poses the question of the significance and position of man. He raises the question with respect to man's relation to God on the one side and all of creation on the other. He goes beyond Ps. 8 in raising the question of the gap between the place promised man and that in which man actually is found. He draws upon the psalmist's awesome picture of the greatness of man in the Creator's plan, with "glory and honor" and "little less than God." (The word is "angels" in Hebrews, following the Septuagint, but *Elohim* in the Hebrew text of Ps. 8. See below.) His emphasis, however, is upon the failure of man in his existential situation to conform to the ideal. Made to rule all that is—except God himself—man is found not actually so to rule.

Comparison of Ps. 8:5a and Heb. 2:7a discloses two seemingly major variations. In the Hebrew text of Ps. 8, man is made "little less than God." Man's nearness to God is stressed, with special attention to the God-like "dominion" given man. Hebrews follows the Septuagint, with two possible variations, depending upon one's understanding of an ambiguity in the Greek text: "for a little while" instead of "little less than" and "lower than the angels" instead of "less than God." The Greek *brachu ti* may intend "a little while" or "a little something." *Brachus* occurs seven times in the New Testament, sometimes with a

temporal force (cf. Luke 22:58; Acts 5:34; 27:28) and sometimes with the quantitative idea of "a little something" (cf. John
6:7; Heb. 13:22). Context does not settle the usage in Heb. 2:7,
9. If the RSV is correct in rendering it "for a little while," the
usage differs from the author's subsequent employment of the
term in Heb. 13:22, where the reference is to the brevity of the
letter, "a little something." This latter is probably intended.

The more significant variation is that between "less than God"
and "lower than the angels." In the Hebrew text of Ps. 8 the term
is *Elohim*. Some would render this "divine," but if the psalmist
is influenced by Gen. 1:26–28, as seems obvious, the rendering
should be "God." Psalm 8 is a hymn chanting the greatness of
Yahweh, creator of heaven and earth. The psalm begins and
closes with the declaration of Yahweh's majesty in all the earth.
Second only to God in acclaim is man, God's vicegerent, to whom
is given dominion over the works of God's hands.

Common to Ps. 8 and Gen. 1:1–6, 26–28, seems to be the vision
of God as overcoming chaos, the waters, and darkness in his work
of creation.[1] The Hebrew word *bara* (Gen. 1:1) does not imply
creation *ex nihilo;* it may be rendered "made" or "formed."
Neither word used in the two accounts of the making of man
implies creation *ex nihilo*. The Priestly writer used *bara* (Gen.
1:27), and the Yahwist used *yasar* (Gen. 2:7), the word used
for a potter's work, seeing man as "shaped" by Yahweh.[2]

Von Rad correctly isolates the emphasis of Gen. 1:2 in observ-
ing that it is upon the fact that God is Lord of the world and not
upon the fact of order out of chaos.[3] He recognizes that the verse
does see preexisting chaos brought to order, but the emphasis is
not upon God as warrior nor as procreator but as creator, of whose
supporting will the cosmos stands permanently in need.[4] He further writes:

> We see here that the theological thought of ch. 1 moves not so
> much between the poles of nothingness and creation as between
> the poles of chaos and cosmos. It would be false to say, however,
> that the idea of the *creatio ex nihilo* was not present at all (v. 1
> stands with good reason before v. 2!), but the actual concern of
> this entire report of creation is to give prominence, form, and

order to creation out of chaos (cf. the fundamental idea of "separating").[5]

God's initial triumph in bringing order (cosmos) out of chaos is then entrusted to man, made in the likeness of God, in particular being "given dominion" over creation. So, the greatness of God and to some lesser extent the greatness of man are both seen in their having dominion over all creation. Man's true dignity and dominion are seen as derived from God, and that picture of the dignity and dominion is set in the framework of the praise of the majesty of God.[6] It is man's great tragedy that he has functioned so poorly with his power to "have dominion" over the works of God's hands. Man has acted uncertainly and inconsistently in this respect. Sometimes he worships the things of creation, and sometimes he despises them. He has gone far to make shambles of that over which he was designed to rule, exploiting, depleting, and polluting much of his world. God brought order (cosmos) out of chaos and then delegated to man the authority and responsibility to rule over it. Man has contributed something to order (cosmos) and much to chaos, through wars, deforestation, poisoning of water and air, slums, etc.

The author of Hebrews follows the Septuagint's "angels," and he has a special interest in angels, so the force of Ps. 8 (and Gen. 1:1–6, 26–28) is somewhat muted, but even so Hebrews retains an emphasis upon the greatness of man in God's design, a greatness actualized only in Christ. The author of Hebrews is more concerned with the gap between man as intended and man as he is and with the achievement of true humanity in Christ than with the original concerns of the psalmist. For our purpose, we shall be concerned with the adaptation and advance made in Hebrews but also with the original emphasis in Ps. 8 (presumably with parallels to Gen. 1:1–6, 26–28) upon man's glory and dominion over nature as derived from his likeness to God and his appointment as God's vicegerent to continue God's triumph over chaos through the responsible use of authority over all the works of God's hands.

Although the Genesis story and Ps. 8 point to dominion as the point of likeness between man and God, a case could be made for love as the point of likeness between man and God. This cannot be "prooftexted" readily, but it has a strong Biblical base. Scripture can say that "God is love" (I John 4:8), but never does it say that God is dominion. It can ascribe power and dominion to God, but it never says that God is power or dominion. God is more than love, and Scripture would never say that love is God; but that God is love reflects solid Biblical perspective and is no isolated proof text.

With the bold affirmation of God as love is the emphatic first commandment, that we are to love God with our whole being, the second commandment being that one is to love neighbor as himself (Deut. 6:5; Lev. 19:18; Matt. 22:37–39; Mark 12:30–33; Luke 10:27). The love (*agapē*) designated here includes feeling but is more. It is a disposition first in God and then from him in man. It is the disposition to relate to another for that one's good, not counting cost or consequences from this radical love. This love may be as unspectacular as routine charity or as dramatic as martyrdom. It is the kind of love that will give a loaf of bread or one's own life (I John 3:16–18).

The fall of man may be seen as the rejection of God's sovereign rule and the assertion by man (Adam) of himself in independence of God. Thus it may be seen as loss of "dominion" on the part of man in the very act of trying to seize it. Viewed in another light, this grasping for power is the opposite of the love which God is and the love which by commandment is to be the law of our lives. The cross, on the other hand, is the ultimate in love, radical self-denial and self-giving. It is only through "dying with Christ" that we begin identifying with the kind of existence that God has (Rom. 6:3–11; Gal. 2:20). The loss of love, then, is the loss of the image of God, and the recovery of love is the recovery of that image.

Dominion and love are not antithetical; they belong together. True dominion is had only in love. God's dominion is the sovereignty of redeeming love (Col. 1:13). He rules by giving and serving. His ultimate triumph is the cross. Nowhere is this sung more clearly than in the poetry of the Apocalypse:

Worthy art thou [Christ] to take the scroll and to open its seals,
for thou wast slain and by thy blood didst ransom men for God
from every tribe and tongue and people and nation
and hast made them a kingdom and priests to our God.
                                                              (Rev. 5:9–10.)

And they have conquered him [the Accuser] by the blood of the Lamb
and by the word of their testimony, for they loved not their lives
        even unto death.
                                                              (Rev. 12:11.)

For God and for man dominion is exercised through the love that
serves even to the point of radical sacrifice. If the image of God
has to do with man's having dominion even as God has dominion,
in the final analysis this dominion is that of triumphant love.

Dominion is not to be confused with tyranny, in God or in man.
God's creative work was an act of dominion, bringing order out
of chaos, a firmament into the seas and light into darkness. But
God's creative work was also an act of submission. It was a re-
linquishing of dominion as well as an act of dominion. In creating
man, God gave up something of his own freedom. God was sovereign enough to do that. God did share his freedom. He did make
man in his own likeness, able to love or to hate, trust or distrust,
live under the sovereignty of God or rebel. Man can say "yes" or
"no" to God, and in so doing he is not merely repeating words
that God puts in his mouth. God was free enough to give man
freedom; and the freedom, once given, is real. God does not pre-
destine how man is to use that freedom. Even God's grace is re-
sistible.

Not only to man did God grant freedom and power, but also to
nature. Although he brought order out of chaos, he did not take
from nature all its own freedom. It, too, has its awesome power of
earthquake and storm, of heat and cold. Nature is even free to de-
velop such forms as mosquitoes and black widow spiders. God is
Lord over the natural world but has not chosen to reduce it to the
status of a gadget. Man, even more so than nature, has his God-
given power and freedom. The ultimate dominion for God and for
man is that of love—persuasive power but not coercive power.

God's dominion is not tyranny over man nor nature. Man's proper dominion is never tyranny but that of the power of responsible love.

The author of Hebrews, after posing the basic problem of the gap between man as intended by the Creator and man as he actually is, moves on to find his answer in Jesus Christ, who through suffering and death is completed (Heb. 2:9 f.). Jesus proves to be true man. Of course, Jesus is to the author far more than man. He is God's Son (Heb. 1:2) and he is the one who "reflects the glory of God and bears the very stamp of his nature" (Heb. 1:3). He apparently sees the Son as actually addressed as "God" (Heb. 1:8). But the author also knows Jesus as a real man, "one who in every respect has been tempted as we are" (Heb. 4:15) and who "in the days of his flesh" prayed "with loud cries and tears" (Heb. 5:7). As man, Jesus is found attaining all the "glory and honor" and the dominion for which man was made but from which destiny he fell miserably short.

Further, the author of Hebrews shows how man's true destiny is reached only as he participates in the triumphant life and death of Christ. He who could "taste death for every one" (Heb. 2:9) was as "the pioneer of their salvation" the one "bringing many sons to glory" (Heb. 2:10). He entered into the "flesh and blood" or the "nature" of men that he might deliver them from their bondage and make them "his brethren" (Heb. 2:14–18). Through suffering he became to all who obey the "cause" of eternal salvation (Heb. 5:9). In Jesus we have a sure and steadfast anchor of the soul, a hope that enters into the inner shrine behind the curtain, where Jesus has gone as a "forerunner" on our behalf (Heb. 6:19 f.). In other words, in him man has his own access into the holy of holies, i.e., into the presence of God (Heb. 9:24). Jesus, the true Man, brings man to God and thus to man's own true destiny under God (Heb. 7:24 f.). We may "have confidence to enter the sanctuary by the blood of Jesus," and that is "by the new and living way which he opened for us through the curtain" (Heb. 10:19 f.). He saves us by writing a new law on our hearts (Heb. 10:16), making for us a fresh and living way to God (Heb. 10:19 f.).

To the author of Hebrews, Jesus Christ is true God and true man. He brings God to man, and only God can mediate God. He brings man to God, himself the first to become fully, truly man and the one in union with whom we may become truly man. In him man reaches his true destiny, becoming truly man in the presence of God. This is the author's answer to the gap between man as envisioned by Ps. 8 and man as he actually is: on the one side, created "little less than God" (or Angels) and to have dominion over all else that is created and on the other side actually more subjected than subjecting, falling short of his authentic being. Jesus Christ is God uniquely present in one who is truly man. In Jesus Christ alone man becomes himself—less than God yet more than all else in creation.

Man's Unique Place

Man is created in the image of God, but he is not God. Man is created and thus a creature, but he is not a mere creature. His position in the design of God is unique, belonging to man alone. That is his glory and also his peril. Man's misery and failure result from his rebellion against his uniqueness, as he seeks to be too much or too little, as he seeks to be God or to be mere creature. He is tempted from both sides, from the side of his kinship to God and from the side of his kinship to all creation. He becomes truly man only as he finds his authentic existence in this polarity between God and creation, akin to each but not identical with either, under the dominion of God (the kingdom of God) but having dominion over all creation. Genesis 1:26 declares God's design for man:

> Then God said, "Let us make man (*adam*) in our image, after our likeness; and let them have dominion over the fish of the sea, and over the birds of the air, and over the cattle, and over all the earth, and over every creeping thing that creeps upon the earth."

Two key words are "image" and "dominion." Man is created in the likeness of God and created to have dominion over all else in creation. It is indispensable to the Biblical view of man that those two polar realities be kept in proper focus and in proper balance.

The Image of God. Precisely what is meant by the image of God is not spelled out in Scripture. Help may come from Gen. 5:3, where it is said that Adam "became the father of a son in his own likeness, after his image." It does not follow necessarily that Seth looked like Adam, but there was an essential kinship between them. Something of Adam lived on in Seth and gave Seth his being. It was a father and son relationship, not just the relationship between a maker and what is made. Adam doubtless *made* various things but he *begot* his son. Genesis does not hold that God begot man, but he did create man in his own image. God has a kinship to man not granted to nature.

God made the world and the plants and animals within it, but only in man did he breathe something of himself, causing man to become "a living being" or "a living soul" (Gen. 2:7). As the relationship between Adam and Seth was personal, between subject and subject, so between God and man. Things are objects but persons are subjects.[7] Man is a part of creation, thus to some extent a thing that is made. But man is more than object, more than thing. A part of man's being in the image of God is that he is a conscious subject, sufficiently akin to God to be able to commune with God and to have dominion over all that is object or thing. We may say that it is in his "spiritual" capacity that man has his likeness to God. We will see later that to Paul "spirit" is the wholeness of man in relationship with God (see Chapter 2), but possibly "personal" comes closer to being the inclusive idea. Only man can enter into an "I-Thou" relationship with God. Man can also enter into an "I-Thou" relationship with his fellowman, and it is only at this level that he is truly man, subject and not object, person and not thing.[8]

Although the personal, I-Thou or Subject-subject relationship between God and man may be a key to the meaning of "the image of God," another clue appears in the context in which the term is introduced as well as in Ps. 8. This is the recognition of the "dominion" assigned to man in creation. That man is to have dominion is stressed both in Gen. 1:26 and Ps. 8:4, in each case following hard upon the recognition that man is made in the image or likeness of God. Moule has sound exegetical ground for concluding: "Perhaps the most satisfying of the many interpretations, both ancient and modern, of the meaning of the image of God in man is that which sees it basically as responsibility." [9]

Moule goes on to observe that, of course, it is responsible authority which is God-like. God has made man sufficiently like himself that man may, and is intended to, exercise responsible authority over all creation. The psalmist, followed by the author of Hebrews, brings into close relationship the two primary factors of man's subjection to God, "a little less than God," and the divine intention that man "have dominion" over all creation. Man's authority to have dominion is much of his likeness to God. This dominion is to be "correlative to man's subjection to God." [10]

As seen above, the particular "dominion" alluded to in Ps. 8 and Gen. 1:1–6, 26–28, seems to be God's triumph over the chaos of floods and darkness, forming the land and the light. This dominion is then entrusted to man, made in the image of God. In this context, man's role is seen as that of ruling all the works of God's hands, remaining subordinate to God alone.

Von Rad cogently observes that the text speaks less of the nature of God's image than of its purpose, with less said of the gift (God's image) than the task (having dominion).[11] He cautions that "the marvel of man's bodily appearance is not at all to be excepted from the realm of God's image" and that "one will do well to split the physical from the spiritual as little as possible," for "the whole man is created in God's image." [12] He concludes that the emphasis is upon man's likeness to God with respect to having dominion:

> Just as powerful earthly kings, to indicate their claim to dominion, erect an image of themselves in the provinces of their empire where they do not personally appear, so man is placed upon earth in God's image as God's sovereign emblem. He is really only God's representative, summoned to maintain and enforce God's claim to dominion over the earth.[13]

What Is Man! This is an exclamation as well as a question. The psalmist (Ps. 8) and the author of Hebrews alike marvel at the attention God gives man. The question, "What is man?" is not raised to disparage him but to contemplate his greatness. What is it about man that causes God to be "mindful of him" and to "care for him"? The psalmist frames the question in a cosmic setting: against the glory of God himself "whose glory above the heavens is chanted" (Ps. 8:1) and against the wonder of the heavens, the moon and the stars (Ps. 8:3). Why does man have so great and so unique a place in all of this?

There is the story of one who had gained his first awareness of the vastness of the universe, with its countless galaxies and seemingly unending expansion. In all this is the tiny earth and upon it man, physically but a tiny speck upon a speck of an earth. Overwhelmed by it all, he said, "Astronomically speaking, man is nothing." To this, someone else had the perception to reply, "Astronomically speaking, man is the astronomer!" What a difference! Judged by the criterion of his size as an object, man is comparatively nothing, a speck of flesh on a speck called earth. But man is not essentially an object among objects; he is a subject made in the image of the Subject and given dominion over all objects that are made.

Thus far in the United States space program, men have landed on the moon five times. What the future holds is beyond anyone's imagination. Man is probing this universe, with telescope and spaceships. Man is studying this vast universe. So far as we know, it is not studying man. Man is looking at it, but as far as we know, it is not looking back at him. We know that men have been on the moon exploring it, but apparently the moon does not know that it is being explored. Neither do the dogs and birds and fish know what is going on. All that is falls into two polar situations, the personal and the thing, subjects and objects. Man, made in the image of God, is personal. He primarily is subject and not object. He may enter into communion with God, and he with God may participate in creativity and in conscious and responsible dominion over all things made.

Neither Genesis nor Ps. 8 explicitly says that God's commission to man to have dominion extends beyond the earth to the larger universe, although this may be implied in Ps. 8. It may also be implied in Heb. 2 :8, "He left nothing outside his control." It certainly does not follow that because man's dominion over the larger sphere is not explicit in the commission that it is invalid. This probably is best understood as simply reflecting the limits of ancient man's grasp of his universe. As late as my own boyhood the expression "Tell it to the man in the moon" was supposed to dismiss a matter as utterly unreal and impossible. Man's dominion over the larger universe is not forbidden or excluded in the divine commission; it is just not explicit. In the long ago space exploration was neither advocated nor prohibited; it was not considered. But surely in principle man's commission to have dominion extends to the larger universe.

One then may be confident that man's quests and conquests on the earth and into the larger universe are proper and within the limits of God's commission to man. This holds true on three conditions: (1) that man not forget God his maker, in whose image he is made but than whom man is less; (2) that man not forget his fellowman, also made in the image of God to be participant in having dominion; and (3) that man not forget that the universe is God's own creation and that it is good. Man may properly go as far as he can in exploration and dominion of the universe, so long as he remembers God the maker of it all and his fellowman (past, present, and future), to whom he is indebted and who is equally precious to God. Of course, it follows that to remember God and mankind one will not construe dominion as the destruction, depletion, or pollution of the universe. There is no ecological threat from any man who sees himself in the image of God and also as his brother's keeper (Gen. 4 :9). To "have dominion" is to exercise responsible authority over things—this in the company of God and other people.

THE IMAGE OF GOD BUT NOT GOD

Man's first blunder was in confusing his being in the image of God with being God. Adam and Eve were not content to be like

God; they sought to be God. They saw God as a limit and as a threat. They saw God as denying their fulfillment by restricting their existence, holding back from them fruit which they needed.

In a sense, Gen., ch. 3, is telling us that man was not content with the uniqueness of his assigned position, in the image of God with dominion over all creation. Man wanted more. He tried to set God aside and replace him with himself. To put it colloquially, man "went for broke." As Principal John Baillie put it in a classroom lecture at New College, Edinburgh: "Man tried to be the whole cheese." Why be "a little less than God" if he could be his own God, answering to no authority above his own will? A faulty self-love, an ill-advised self-trust, and a woeful misunderstanding of his own identity and destiny came to tragic expression in man's self-assertion against God. Refusing to find his true existence under God, he sought it in independence of God. His idolatry was that he tried to be God. What is known as the fall of man "was basically a venture into autonomy," [14] and the venture proved to be counterproductive, yielding bondage and not freedom, ruin and not fulfillment.

Paul in his own way tells the same story as is found in Genesis (cf. Rom. 1:18–32). Both accounts tell of man's self-destruction in the very attempt at self-salvation. The difference is that Gen., ch. 3, puts it in the form of a story that a child can understand unless confused by the learned theologizing of an adult mind that has lost its childhood imagination, whereas Paul writes more prosaically in the essay style of a professor. The parallels are striking; in form they differ, but in analysis of the human predicament they are together.

The Wrath of God. Romans 1:18–32 is the only place in Scripture where "the wrath of God" is pursued as a subject in itself. Paul clearly indicates what it is, its causal factors, nature, and consequences. There is not a trace of apocalyptic imagery or thought in the passage. There is not a hint of arbitrary or external punishment. The wrath of God is God's delivering man over to himself when man chooses to have his own way. The wrath of God is the working out of man's own pseudoexistence—when man refuses to know God and takes things into his own hands, when man tries to be autonomous, a law to himself.

That the wrath is man's responsibility and not God's is indicated in Paul's claim that God makes himself knowable to man, offering to man the relationship out of which come the necessary resources for authentic existence. It is not that man is left to his own resources or that man must bear the responsibility for finding God. Man is "without excuse," for God has made himself knowable "since the creation of the world," able to be "perceived in the things that have been made" (Rom. 1:20). "The things that have been made" could be rendered "the things done." In his doing or making, God from the beginning of creation has made something of himself knowable. Paul does not remotely hint that God gives enough knowledge to some to damn them but not enough to save them. That "damnable theology" is not Biblical. Nothing in the passage supports any conclusion except that man is responsible only within the limits of his ability to respond. He is responsible for the light he has. Paul indicates that men are not condemned for the limited light they have but for the rejection of that light.

Romans 1:28 is the key to the wrath suffered by man: "Since they did not see fit to acknowledge God, God gave them up to a base mind." (RSV). In Greek there is a play on words hard to capture in English translation. Closer to the idea is this: "Because they did not approve (*edokimasan*) to know God, God delivered them over to an unproven (*adokimon*) mind." The word *dokimazein* suggests the idea of proving by test. Its cognate *adokimos* designates what has failed the test. Man put the knowledge of God to the test and failed it; man judged that he is better off not entering into a relationship of personal knowledge with God. In "flunking" God, man actually "flunked" himself. It was not that "the knowledge of God" was proven deficient but that man's mind failed. God turned man over to his own mind, which had failed the test.

Implied throughout is the primary truth that God offers himself to man but never forces himself upon man. God opens up to man the possibility of a personal relationship of mutual trust, but this is never coercive upon man. God never retracts the freedom given man in creation. God never destroys his own creature by turning a subject into an object, a person into a thing. God does not in the name of salvation rob man of that which is given him in creation, the image of God in man which, whatever else it means, means that man must find his existence within the framework of freedom. Man cannot enter into authentic existence apart from God, apart from taking God into his knowledge; but neither can this be imposed upon man. The fallacy inherent in "predestination" is that it would be damnation raised to the nth degree, not salvation at the personal level. Things may be managed, manipulated, coerced; man may not be manipulated if he is to remain man.

Paul three times says that "God gave them up" (Rom. 1:24, 26, 28). Gave them up to whom or to what? God gave men up to themselves, to their own deliberate choices. What else can God do if he respects the freedom given man from the beginning? The calculated risk in making man in his own image was that man might abuse that freedom. But to this there was no alternative, if man was to be created at all, made in the image of God. One may ask why God would create man in a freedom fraught with such peril. One may also ask why a husband and wife deliberately bring into the world a baby who may be born physically defective, mentally retarded, or who may grow up to be criminal. The answer is that parents at their best choose to run this risk because of the possibility that the child may be sound and beautiful in body, mind, and personal development. Personal existence, for God and man, has its inbuilt risks; and God himself could not escape those risks. God could make things without risk, for they can be coerced. Persons he could make possible only at the risk of "wrath," the ruin that overtakes man and society when God-given freedom is abused.

Paul goes a step farther in describing the working out of "the wrath of God." He pictures this in terms of the breakdown of the individual person (Rom. 1:24–27) and the breakup of the human family (Rom. 1:28–32). The former he illustrates in terms of man's self-ruin as what was made to be a man turns out to be just a "male" or a "female" (Paul normally does not use these biological terms for men and women), and as even this falls short of the sexual fulfillment possible between man and woman when it breaks down into homosexual expression. Seeking to become God, man becomes biology. Falling short of wholeness, man becomes a fraction, a fragment, a torso. Rejecting the knowledge of God, man sinks down into his creaturehood and distorts that.

In the concluding paragraph (Rom. 1:28–32), Paul sketches the antisocial vices that destroy the human family. Cut off from God, man cuts himself off not only from his own authentic self but from his fellowman. Adam and Eve refuse to know God in a relationship of trust; then they accuse one another, and next Cain kills Abel. This in brief is the story of man's self-ruin. This is "the wrath of God," not of an angry God throwing thunderbolts but of a faithful God refusing to coerce man, even if man chooses the way of ruin in the quest for fulfillment, death in the quest for life, bondage in the quest for freedom. The "wrath of God" means that God takes man's freedom so seriously that he permits man to self-destruct if man so chooses.[15]

Paul specifies that in refusing to know God, man "exchanged the glory of the immortal God for images resembling mortal man or birds or animals or reptiles" (Rom. 1:23). Sometimes man's idolatry projects itself in the shape of some creature about him. His basic idolatry is the worship of himself. From Adam to us, we are tempted on one side of our existence to become God. Made in his image, we try to be more, to be God. This is set forth by the writer of Genesis and by Paul, each in his own way.

The Marred Image. In Biblical teaching the image of God was not completely destroyed, as some theologians have had it. This is especially obvious if the "image" has special reference to man's having "dominion" over the works of God's hands. Man in his lowest depravity has not lost power to dominate. Neither has he completely lost his moral sense, his power to distinguish between right and wrong. Further, he has not lost his power to hear God and respond to him. The early Barthian view that the image of God was completely destroyed by the fall of man and that nothing remained in man which God could address (*Ansprechbarkeit*), nothing in man upon which God could take hold (*Anknüpfungspunkt*), is unsupported in the Bible and in human experience. Throughout Scripture, God is seen as addressing man as he is, holding sinful man responsible for his response to the word of God. Man does remain addressable. He is responsible. He can yet say "yes" or "no" to God. The image of God in man has been marred but not removed.

This conclusion is sustained in the account of the birth of Seth, where it is said that Adam "became the father of a son *in his own likeness, after his image,* and named him Seth" (Gen. 5:3; italics added). Thus Adam is seen as passing on to Seth the divine likeness in which he was created, and this was after the Fall.[16]

What is taught in Scripture is not that through sin man completely loses the image of God but that these powers in man which give him his potential God-likeness are blunted, distorted, or so damaged that they do not function freely and reliably as they ought. This is what Paul means by "the wrath of God." He puts it this way: "They became futile in their thinking and their senseless minds were darkened" (Rom. 1:21). Refusing to know God, they brought upon themselves a progressive deterioration of their moral sense.

A classic treatment of the power of sin to blunt man's perceptive powers is found in the story of Jesus' healing of a man born blind (John, ch. 9). Having given the man eyes of flesh which could see, Jesus offered himself as the light of the world, offering the eyes of faith to any who would receive them. Some of the religious leaders protested the fact that Jesus had healed the blind man on the Sabbath. Their concern was more for the *things* of religion than for persons. When they stubbornly rejected the light Jesus offered them, Jesus made this startling proclamation:

> For judgment I came into this world, that those who do not see may see, and that those who see may become blind. (John 9:39.)

Jesus meant that he came to give sight to those who needed it and who would receive it. But those who rejected the light would do more than reject the light. They would thus put out their power to see. To refuse to see is ultimately to destroy within oneself the power to see. To close one's eyes is not to put out the light but to put out one's sight.

This is "the wrath of God," not an angry God's hurling of thunderbolts but the deadening, enslaving force of sin taken into one's being. It is not that the first man committed one act of sin and as a result the whole human race came under God's judgment or lost the divine image (see Chapter 3 for discussion of Rom. 5:12 and I Cor. 15:22). It is that the image of God is marred, vision blurred, hearing blunted, and hearts hardened to the extent that man closes his eyes to God's light, his ears to God's word, his heart to God's love.

Man, then, never completely loses the image of God within himself, but it can be so blunted that one ceases to function as true man. He can go so far in rejecting truth and light that he can scarcely tell the difference between light and darkness, truth and falsehood, good and evil. The cold is physically painful to a point, then numbness settles in and one does not feel the cold. He is least aware of the cold when he is coldest. So it is with the awful power of sin to blunt the very powers in us that set us apart as made in the image of God.

Man's Idolatries. The essence of man's idolatry, his effort to become God, is his disposition to give ultimate authority to his own will, answering to no higher claim than his own will. With this may be an exaggerated sense of one's own wisdom and goodness.

The Book of Job deals extensively with subtle forms of man's attempt to "be God." [17] In particular, it shows how man may victimize even himself, as when he pretends to have the wisdom and integrity to rule on his own existence. This subtle idolatry is reflected in Job's outburst as he curses the day of his birth, judging his own life as though it were nothing (Job, ch. 3; see also ch. 7). Again, Job illustrates man's proneness to idolatry when in legal fashion he challenges God, as though he had the wisdom and goodness for that (Job, chs. 29 to 31). In chs. 38 to 39, God challenges Job to show that he *knows* enough to take over God's function in judgment (as Job does in ch. 3). In chs. 40 to 41, God challenges Job to show that he is *strong* enough to carry through such pretension. In ch. 28 it is shown that neither wisdom nor understanding is inherent in man.

From the arrogance of thus lifting oneself to the height that belongs alone to God comes also the arrogance of coercing and exploiting other people and the abuse of God's world through depleting it, polluting it, and destroying its order and beauty. This is not only idolatry, but it is a falsification of the nature of God as well as the identity of God. When man plays God, the god he reflects is false. God does not destroy man nor nature. He does not coerce or use. Only phony, man-made gods do that.

Man's idolatry appears wherever man treats his fellowman as an object: a slave to be bought and sold, a servant to be used, a thing to be manipulated, or a nobody to be ignored or neglected.

One form of idolatry that has plagued religion, including Christendom, is that of thinking that one so fully possesses the truth that he has the right to force it upon others. This reaches its ultimate arrogance when any individual person or human structure, religious or otherwise, claims infallibility for itself. This is rank idolatry. Out of this illusion or pretension to infallibility comes "the temptation which suggests that man—other men—can and must be managed and manipulated." [18] Hence come such atrocities as religious persecution, heresy hunts, inquisitions, the Crusades, religious indexes, book burnings, etc. The arrogant claim that "heresy has no rights" roots in the idolatrous claim to one's own infallible judgment as to what is truth and what is heresy. With the conceit of infallibility is also that of self-righteousness, as though one were good enough to rule another, denying him even the freedom of conscience or speech.

Possibly man's most frightening idolatry appears in his corporate efforts, the mad mob or the totalitarian state. Any totalitarianism is idolatrous. When the state claims ultimate authority it presumes to be God. This is true of Fascism, Communism, and all dictator regimes. "Caesar" or the state has a proper place only when "Caesar" is himself submissive to God and respectful of the dignity and freedom of man made in the image of God (cf. Rom., ch. 13). When the state makes ultimate demands it becomes the Beast (Rev., ch. 13). The validity of "civil disobedience" emerges at just this point. Biblical evidence is solid on the side of refusal of ultimate authority to any human structure, whether political or religious (cf. Daniel, Stephen, Peter, Paul, the Seer of the Apocalypse). Bunyan, Niemöller, and others less well known have followed in this noble tradition.

Well-meaning people encourage idolatry whenever they so join together "God and Country" that one cannot be served without the other. This not only raises country to a totalitarian status —making it omnipotent, if not the embodiment of all goodness— but it makes country divine. It is poor patriotism to withhold loyal dissent and criticism, and it is idolatry so to misread "Render therefore to Caesar the things that are Caesar's and to God the things that are God's" (Matt. 22:21) as to make Caesar independent of God or the peer of God.

Religion aids and abets this corporate idolatry wherever it identifies itself with culture. The church itself is constantly tempted so to identify itself with some nation that it adopts the values of that culture and leaves unchallenged injustice, arrogance, and exploitation. Tillich describes this danger as that of worshiping the gods of space instead of the God of time.[19] This is man's tendency to worship a god limited to tribal or national boundaries. The gods of space (national or territorial gods) necessarily destroy justice. Under its god of space, a national group so exercises its will to power that it denies justice to those outside its spatial boundaries. It can also deny justice to minority groups within its own boundaries. This became grotesque under Nazism, when various churches, Catholic and Protestant, bowed the knee to Hitler with a view to their own survival or enhancement. Less apparent yet not less real is this idolatry wherever a church fails to stand free of all human structures, answering ultimately to God alone.

CREATURE BUT NOT MERE CREATURE

God created man, so man is a creature. He is a creature, but more. Man is created in the image of God. Though not God, neither is he fully, exhaustively, or exclusively identified with the creation. Man bridges the gap between God and creation, unique in his kinship to both. It is as fatal to man to see himself as only a part of nature as to aspire to be God.

As seen above, the image of God which man bears is closely related to his commission to have dominion over creation. This is emphatic in Gen. 1:26 f.:

> Then God said, "Let us make man *in our image, after our likeness;* and let them *have dominion* over the fish of the sea, and over the birds of the air, and over the cattle, and over all the earth, and over every creeping thing that creeps upon the earth." So God created man *in his own image,* in *the image of God* he created him. (Italics added.)

Brought together here and elsewhere (cf. Ecclus. 17:1–4; Ps. 8:4–8) are two primary ideas, man's being made in the image of God and man's being given dominion over all else that is made. As seen already, whatever else "the image of God" may imply, it at least includes and stresses responsibility and authority, God-like, responsible authority.[20] This responsible authority is to be exercised over nature, and it is to be "correlative to man's subjection to God." [21] Consistent with the whole Biblical perspective, man's unique position is bounded on one side by God with whom he has a unique kinship but to whom he must ever be subordinate ("a little less than God") and on the other side by nature, with which he has an essential kinship ("created" and "formed of dust from the ground") but over which he must "have dominion."

Man is both to rule and be ruled. He is to rule nature but be under the rule (kingdom) of God. It is his tragic record that he has rebelled against the rule or kingdom of God, and he has found himself actually in bondage to nature, more ruled by it than ruling it. Man's bondage to all over which he was created to have dominion may be expressed in many ways, as when man is ruled by forces within his own body or by forces without.

The Human Body. One may readily think of appetites and impulses within the natural body as often being man's actual rulers. Man may indeed be ruled by appetite for food or drink or by the sexual drive written deep in his nature. But these are by no means the extent of the threats to his freedom. His bondage may go far beyond that of gluttony or sex. Man may be enslaved by lust, greed, fear, envy, jealousy, prejudices, anxiety, hate, or even something as noble as work. He may become a "workaholic" as easily as an addict to alcohol or drugs.[22]

Nowhere in Scripture is the human body itself seen as evil. This is a pagan concept, held by Gnostics and others; but it is not Biblical. In Biblical teaching, God created the heavens and the earth and all that is in them. He formed man's own body from the dust of the earth and breathed into it something of himself, thus making man a living soul (a living being). Body belongs essentially to what man is. Body belongs to man as created and to man as redeemed. Body belongs essentially to man beyond physical death, and this is why resurrection (bodily existence) and not immortality (disembodied soul) is the Biblical teaching. Whatever may be the difference between the "physical body" that is "sown" and the "spiritual body" that is "raised" (I Cor. 15:42–50), it is a body. Scripture knows nothing of man as a disembodied spirit or a naked soul. It is pagan and not Biblical to see man as only "spirit" or "soul," caught temporarily in a body viewed as the "tomb" or "prison" of the soul from which soul is to be delivered by death. To Scripture, death is "the last enemy" (I Cor. 15:26) and it is to be defeated (I Cor. 15:54–57). Death is not the "friend" that liberates "soul" or "spirit" from body.

With the pagan low view of the body is the equally pagan idea that the appetites of the body are themselves evil. Hence arise restrictions against food and sex, restrictions on ascetic grounds. Not to be confused with asceticism are various bodily disciplines for health or vocational reasons. For example, vocational celibacy is the surrender of marriage as something good in favor of (for some people) more freedom for vocational ministry. Here sex within marriage is seen as good, not evil. It is surrendered only in favor of some other proper claim. To the contrary, celibacy on ascetic grounds sees sex as evil within itself.

Man is to "have dominion" and this includes dominion over his own body. He is to rule and not be ruled by bodily appetite, urge, or impulse. Of course, it is not simply over the physical body that he is to have dominion. It is over himself. Man is to be under control. It is not without significance that "self-control" is included in "the fruit of the Spirit" (Gal. 5:22). Man in all the many aspects of his selfhood is to be under control. In one sense, this is self-control, one's "having dominion" over himself. Of course, this having dominion is to be correlative with man's subjection to God.

Materialism. The material in general is no more evil than is the physical body in particular. But though the material is not evil, materialism is evil. To give ultimate worth or power to the material is materialism. This is a form of idolatry. Jesus had much to say about money and about the importance of food, clothing, and shelter, universal concerns of mankind. Chiefly, Jesus was concerned to free man from the tyranny of things (cf. Matt. 6:19–34; 19:16–30; Luke 12:13–21). He saw that man could be ruled by the very things he was commissioned to rule. Only as freed from the tyranny of things is man able to put things to their proper use, to the service of himself, of his fellowman, and of God.

It is significant that Jesus warned, "You cannot serve God and mammon" (Matt. 6:24). He did not say, "God and Satan." Mammon, hoarded wealth, is the "god" that tends to have dominion over us. One can be deceived as to his relationship to the material. He may be owned by what he thinks he owns. This is the point of the story of the prosperous farmer, the "rich fool" who dreamed of a retirement which he never enjoyed (Luke 12:13–21). He thought that he owned a farm but it owned him. He spoke of "my crops," "my barns," and "my soul," but he found out too late that he owned or controlled nothing. He belonged to what he thought he ruled. The Greek of Luke 12:20 is ambiguous, but the subject is plural, not singular: "This night *they* are requiring your soul of you." "They" could refer to the crops and barns to which he had lost his freedom.

One hears it said, "I can't get away from the office," or it may be "the store," "the study," or "the farm." Why can he not get away? Does he mind the store or does it mind him? One may be enslaved in bondage to his work or to the material gains he seeks to derive from his work. To bury one's heart in perishable things is to perish with them (Matt. 6:19–21). Stinginess (or envy) is blindness, the eye that is not sound (Matt. 6:23) ;[23] anxiety over things is unnecessary; it is unprofitable; and it is evil (Matt. 6:25–34). The only alternative to the tyranny of things is the kingdom (sovereign rule) of God (Matt. 6:33). It is only as man submits to the sovereignty of God that he can fulfill his God-given commission to "have dominion" over creation.

Mere Creature. In various ways man is tempted to sink down into his creaturehood and be no more than a creature among the creatures. Man's likeness to the lower animals is obvious: his bodily form, his needs for food and drink, his mortality, etc. If one sets out to list parallels between man and beast, the chore is an easy one. Man can forget his dissimilarity to the lower animal as he concentrates upon the similarity. He can see himself as mere animal and be content to take his place among the beasts as just another animal, even if a higher animal.

One may be tempted to yield to what he sees as his biological destiny. This may take shape in terms of surrender to bodily claims as ultimate. One may know no law higher than that of "biological destiny." When an animal is hungry, he eats. When the sex impulse is awakened, it seeks fulfillment. It is that simple. When man sees himself as just another animal, the logic is simple. Life is seen as just living. One is to "be natural." His song becomes, "I eat when I'm hungry, and I drink when I'm dry." Thus to absolutize the physical body and its appetites is as dehumanizing as to follow the Gnostic fallacy that the body is evil and is to be denied. The "naturalist" gives the physical body ultimate claim and this is idolatry. He makes a god of the physical body. The Gnostic sees the body as evil. He makes a devil of it. Both are wrong, and each dehumanizes man. One elevates the part to the position of the whole. The other would discard the part altogether.

Secularism. The term "secular" is Latin, *saeculum,* apparently referring to race, age, or world. Whatever its precise derivation, it is concerned with limits, whether time or sphere or whatever. From Biblical perspective, the fallacy of secularism is its confusion of the part with the whole. It is not concern with temporal or spatial or with the material or physical that is wrong. It is wrong to be indifferent to the temporal, spatial, physical, or material. But it is idolatry to raise any one of these to ultimacy. It is to dehumanize man to find his identity with these alone.

Man must find meaning within the time-space continuum and with respect to the physical and material. To be rejected is the Gnostic or pagan illusion of man as pure spirit whose "fall" is his historical-bodily existence and whose salvation is his escape from "matter." But also to be rejected is the secularism that decries the world of spirit or man's essential kinship to God.

THE POLAR TENSION

We have been conditioned to think of tension as bad, and we dream of a tension-free existence. But the point of this chapter and of this book is that we can find our authentic existence only in polar situations with their inescapable tension. There are tensions that are not compatible with our fulfillment as human beings, and we may be broken or destroyed under improper tensions or under tensions to which we improperly relate. But there are tensions which are proper to human fulfillment. One such tension is that in which we necessarily find our existence in our polar relationship with God and with creation. In all authentic human existence the tension is there and will remain. It is a tension on one side between man and God and on the other side between man and creation.

Salvation is not escape from the tensions of our polar situation. Salvation is in the making to the extent that we properly see, understand, accept, and cultivate these polarities of our human existence. We are created in God's image, but we are not God. We fatally err if we deny God or if we in any sense try to be God. Atheism is fatal, and practical atheism is a greater threat than theoretical atheism. Atheism is the fallacy of denying God, whether philosophically or existentially. But to raise ourselves to the level of deity is likewise fatal to human fulfillment. Man is "lost" as man if he tries to be God, and he is fragmentized if he tries to be man without God.

On the side of our creaturehood the tension likewise remains. We are created but we are not just creatures. We are created to have dominion and cannot become truly human apart from responsible dominion. To sink down into our creaturehood as though we were nothing but creatures or to sink down below creation as we worship the creature in any form is fatal to our humanity.

Our position is unique. It is a polar situation: man is like God but not God, created but more than creature. Man is man—nothing more and nothing less. He was created to be man and he is to be saved as man. Salvation is not becoming an angel, not becoming a naked spirit, not becoming an animal, not anything except becoming a human being. This is true "humanism" and it is Biblical from Genesis through Revelation.

Man has been created to exercise responsible dominion. Responsibility and authority are properly related to one another by principle, not irresponsibly or arbitrarily. There can be no fulfillment of responsibility without that particular authority necessary to such fulfillment. Authority is to be matched to a given responsibility, neither more nor less and not other than that authority required by a given responsibility.

A case in point will serve to illustrate. Four people may be motoring through the country together. The person at the steering wheel at a given time may or may not be the best driver in the group, but given the responsibility of the wheel he has to have the authority over it if he is to discharge his responsibility. But the proper authority over the steering wheel does not imply extension of authority into other matters, e.g., the choice of a menu at lunch time. Being the driver and having its corresponding authority does not mean that one has the authority to choose what his traveling companions are to eat at mealtime. That authority might belong to one's physician to whom one has entrusted the responsibility for his health, but not to the driver as driver of the automobile.

God has created man in his own likeness, in the likeness of him who brought order out of floods and darkness. Man does have God-likeness and his assigned sphere of dominion. Man does not have responsibility or authority for being God, and it is not his proper role to play God. Neither is he given God-like authority over man, his brother. He is given dominion over the natural order. His ecological function is to move along the lines of his Creator God, who brought light into darkness and who formed a cosmos out of chaos. Whenever man is willing to accept his true identity and role—God-like but not God, creature but more—he may continue God's creative work and know the joyous fulfillment of an authentic humanity. When man learns to be subordinate to the rule (kingdom) of God he will learn to have dominion over the works of his hands.

Chapter 2

ASPECTIVE
YET HOLISTIC

The polarities of man's existence include the "poles" of his complexity on the one side and his unitary or holistic nature on the other. Man is highly complex, as multifaceted as a diamond. He may be seen in multiple aspects: physical and psychological, sensuous, rational, volitional, emotional, aesthetic, moral, social, and far more. On the other hand, man is unitary or holistic. He cannot be divided into separable parts. He is aspective but not partitive. For purposes of analysis, he may be seen in terms of what we call feeling, will, or reason, but these cannot be extracted from his being or existence. These cannot be exhibited in isolation one from the other. Neither is man to be reduced to a body-soul dichotomy or a body-soul-spirit (or body-mind-spirit) trichotomy.

We cannot extract, e.g., pure feeling unmixed with reason or will from selfhood. We cannot break up personal selfhood into parts, isolating pure reason from feeling or volition. We cannot exhibit a pound of feeling, a square foot of reason, or six inches of volition. What we label as such are our abstractions, but they cannot actually be extracted. They do not inhere in selfhood in the manner that they appear in our descriptive analysis.

The Hebrew-Christian Scriptures know nothing about relegating sin to some "nonessential" part of the self involved in physical necessity, as in rationalistic and mystic dualism, over against the "true" self of spirit; nor do they know anything about redemption as extracting the "true" self of soul or spirit from the "nonessential" self. The Biblical stance sees man as a unity of spirit and body, emphasized in man's relationship to God both as creator and as redeemer. It sees man standing in the "paradoxical juxtaposition" of being in the "image of God" and yet under judgment as "man the sinner." [1] Sin belongs not to some isolable part of man's selfhood, but rather it arises at the heart of his being and penetrates every aspect of his existence. Correspondingly, salvation must be effected at the center of his being, at the point of his God-given, responsible freedom; and it must be the kind of salvation that penetrates every aspect of his existence. This has far-reaching implications for "ministry," active concern for all men and for the well-being of each man in the totality of his ecological existence.

Apparent Dichotomy or Trichotomy in Scripture

There are passages in the Bible which seem to reflect a partitive view of man, dichotomous or trichotomous. One such passage is from Paul: "May the God of peace himself sanctify you wholly; and may your spirit and soul and body be kept sound and blameless at the coming of our Lord Jesus Christ" (I Thess. 5:23). Special pleading is not in order here, and it is to be admitted that the intention may be trichotomous. However, in the absence of significant supporting evidence, it is proper to look for alternative meaning. The form is trichotomous, but it probably reflects not Paul's deliberate theology but rather the traditional (liturgical) language of the day.[2] The piling up of the three terms (spirit, soul, body) serves only to add emphasis to the phrase "you wholly." The words *holoteleis* ("wholly") and *holoklēron* ("whole in every part") point to the real meaning.[3]

A possible dichotomous trace in Paul may be found in his boast that the woman who forgoes marriage remains undistracted in her concern to be "holy in body and spirit" (I Cor. 7:34). The form is dichotomous, but there is little if any support for this as theologically deliberate. A similar plea in II Cor. 7:1 is for cleansing from all defilement of "flesh and spirit." This appears in what may be an interpolated paragraph (II Cor. 6:14 to 7:1), probably from a lost Pauline letter (cf. I Cor. 5:9). Again, a partitive idea is possible, but without supporting evidence it probably is to be understood as reflecting only traditional language.

Paul's absence in "body" but presence in "spirit" (I Cor. 5:3) is probably to be understood as no more dichotomous than when we use such terminology. He did not mean that he was in Corinth as a ghostly self but simply that he was there in thought and concern.

In the "great commandment" we encounter what on the surface appears to be a polychotomous view of man; but because of the multiple occurrence of the commandment in the Old and New Testaments, it is more open to testing than are the Pauline passages just noted. The great commandment appears in Deut. 6:5; Matt. 22:37; Mark 12:30, 33; and Luke 10:27. Only Luke and Mark agree in their combination of terms (but not even they agree in the order of terms). The Septuagint differs from the Hebrew text; no two Synoptics fully agree with Deuteronomy or with one another; and Mark differs from himself within a single paragraph.[4] It is obvious that precise use of terms was not a concern of the writers. The basic idea is uniform to them, the wholeness or entirety of man given in love to God. The terms do not represent parts of man, but man in his entirety.

In his study of Paul's use of "terms for the inner man" (*psychē, nous, noēma, kardia, pneuma, suneidēsis, dianoia, splagchna, phrenes*), Kümmel finds that these terms "do not denote psychologically different functions, but are used promiscuously."[5]

New Testament Terms for Man

Many terms are used in Scripture to stress the aspective nature of man, man as seen from various perspectives. These terms are not employed consistently. A term may vary in meaning from passage to passage by the same author. Only context can disclose its intention in a given usage. Any one of the terms may be used for the whole man, seen from a given perspective. To the more significant of the terms we now turn.

Psychē. This term is used variously in the New Testament for "soul," "life," "mind," "heart," "self." It translates the Hebrew *nephesh* with closely paralleled usage. It is a term widely misunderstood, for to many it connotes the Platonic idea of an "immortal soul" as sharply distinguished from the body. Under a misunderstanding of the term, many have speculated as to the location of the soul within the body. At this writing there has been a major news release about a group that will try to photograph (infrared, etc.) the soul as it leaves a dying person! This view is close to Orphic religion and Greek philosophy but it woefully misunderstands Scripture—to the detriment of doctrines of man, sin, salvation, ministry, and much else.

The RSV retains "soul" as the translation for *psychē* about 45 times and properly so. The question is, what is meant by "soul"? We already have examined a few passages where the literary form is dichotomous (I Cor. 5:3; 7:34; II Cor. 7:1) or trichotomous (I Thess. 5:23) or even polychotomous (the great commandment). A few others may imply a partitive view. In Matt. 10:28 Jesus warns against the one who can "destroy both soul and body in hell." In the Lukan parallel (Luke 12:4 f.) there is no mention of "soul," and the contrast is between who can only kill the body and the one who can kill and cast into hell. Probably the Matthean version is not to be pressed for a dichotomous conception; it is completely absent in Luke.

In I Peter 2:11 there is a warning against "the passions of the flesh that wage war against your soul." We shall see presently that "flesh" can be used for any aspect of selfhood or for the whole person in his distance from God or in hostility to God. Probably the warning here parallels Paul's distinction between "flesh" and "spirit." In Heb. 4:12 there is reference to the power of the word of God to pierce "to the division of soul and spirit." If pressed, this could reflect a trichotomy in which spirit is encased in soul and both in body, but there is no supporting evidence for this view in Hebrews. Probably the language is traditional and the intention only to stress the awesome power of God to know us through and through.

The term *psychē* is employed over 40 times in the New Testament for "life" (cf. Matt. 2:20, where Herod has sought the child's life, and Rev. 8:9, where the reference is to every creature having life). Often the reference is clearly to life as over against death (cf. Acts 20:10). Sometimes *psychē* wavers between "life" and "self" as in Luke 9:24 f., where one who "loses his life" (Luke 9:24) "loses or forfeits himself" (Luke 9:25). *Psychē* is used a number of times for "mind," in the sense of attitude or disposition (cf. Acts 4:32; 14:2; 15:24; Phil. 1:27). It can also refer to the "heart" (cf. Eph. 6:6; Col. 3:23), much as we speak of doing or saying something "from the heart" or "heartily." Paul no more intended "heart" in the literal sense than we do when we act or speak "from the heart." Here *psychē* connotes genuineness or sincerity.

Most significantly, *psychē* is used at least as often for "self" as with any other meaning in the New Testament. *Psychē* for "self" is a normal usage, a clear warning against any seriously partitive view of selfhood. Some such usages are completely unambiguous, the context being decisive. For example, there were three thousand "souls" added to the church on the day of Pentecost (Acts 2:41). These were persons, not "immortal souls" in the Greek sense. Joseph brought his father Jacob and seventy-five "souls" into Egypt (Acts 7:14). He did not leave their bodies in Canaan. There were two hundred and seventy-six "souls" in the storm-imperiled ship with Paul (Acts 27:37). It was in their bodily existence that they were imperiled, but they are called "souls." The RSV correctly reads that eight "persons" were saved in Noah's ark (I Peter 3:20), although the term is *psychē*. The rich farmer dreams of crops and barns so big that he can say to his *psychē*, "Soul, you have ample goods laid up for many years; take your ease, eat, drink, and be merry" (Luke 12:19). What kind of soul is it that can eat, drink, and be merry? A soul is a self, a person. In Rom. 2:9 every "human being" who does evil and suffers for it is a *psychē*, and in Rom. 13:1 every "person" to be subjected to persons who govern is likewise a *psychē*. The whole man sins and the whole man is called to responsible citizenship. Paul, true to his Hebrew heritage, here thinks of man as a unity. *Psychē* can designate the total self, as when we say, "I got to church early and there wasn't a soul there."

The Biblical teaching is not that one has a soul but that he is a soul. God formed man from "the dust from the ground"; and when he breathed into his nostrils the breath of life, "man became a living being" (Gen. 2:7). The Hebrew word is *nephesh,* rendered *psychē* in Greek. Paul writes that "the first man Adam became a living being" (I Cor. 15:45). "Living being" translates *psychēn zōsan.*

The whole person is soul. What is lost in sin is soul as self, the whole self. To save a soul is to save a person. What survives death is not an "immortal soul" in the Greek sense but a self, a person, a bodily self. When Peter applied Ps. 16:10 to Jesus, "For thou wilt not abandon my soul to Hades" (Acts 2:27), he was declaring the *resurrection* of Jesus. He was not saying that death freed the "soul" of Jesus from the body. He was declaring that the whole person was raised from the dead. "Soul" here is self, a bodily self. Orphic and Platonic ideas of a preexistent soul or a disembodied soul are absent from the New Testament. Body and soul are never set in a truly dualistic opposition to one another.

It remains to be observed that New Testament writers could think of man as *pyschikos,* as natural man, i.e., man apart from the Spirit of God. Paul contrasts the *psychikos* man from the one who receives the Spirit of God (I Cor. 2:14), but it is the whole man who is so designated. The "natural" man is the "unspiritual" man (RSV). In this there is no hint of restriction to a part of man. The same term is used for the "physical" body (I Cor. 15:44, 46). James (3:15) uses it for "unspiritual" wisdom, i.e., wisdom apart from God. Jude (v. 19) uses it for "worldly" people, i.e., the unregenerate. In each instance *psychikos* designates the whole man, with no dichotomous or partitive implication.

Sōma. The word *sōma* appears in eighteen New Testament

writings and may uniformly be translated "body," although with different connotations. It is used normally for the living, visible body, but on occasion even for a corpse (cf. Luke 17:37; Acts 9:40). It is mortal (Rom. 6:12), but it is also redeemable in terms of resurrection (Rom. 8:23; I Cor. 15:35–58), the ultimate goal of God's redeeming action.[6] The body is not evil as such, but it is susceptible to evil (Rom. 6:12). It may also be sanctified to God and as an instrument of righteousness (Rom. 12:1; I Cor. 6:13–20; 7:34). The term may be used for the whole man. Its most prominent use is for the church, the body of Christ, especially in I Corinthians, Romans, and Ephesians.

The original and basic usage of *sōma* is for the natural body. There is not a hint that it is inherently or necessarily evil. Nowhere is the King James Version more misleading than in its rendering "our vile body" (Phil. 3:21) for "our lowly body" (*tapeinōsis* connotes humbleness). There is no Gnostic or puritanical despising of the body in the New Testament. Its mortality and susceptibility to sin are declared, but it may also be "the temple of the Holy Spirit" (I Cor. 6:19). The body may be given degradingly to fornication, but in intention the body is for the Lord and the Lord for the body (I Cor. 6:13). God may be glorified through the body (I Cor. 6:20).

Although "body" designates man aspectively, in his most obvious appearance, the term does not imply a dichotomous or partitive view of man. Man does not have a body; he is a body.[7] This may be demonstrated from the interchange of "your bodies," "your members," and "yourselves" in Rom. 6:12 f. It may be seen also in I Corinthians in a comparison of "your bodies are members of Christ" (I Cor. 6:15) with "you are the body of Christ" (I Cor. 12:27). There is only an apparent contrast with "soul" in I Thess. 5:23; I Cor. 5:3; 7:34. One's body is oneself. To present "your bodies" to God is to present yourselves in bodily existence (Rom. 12:1). Just as one *is* a soul, so he *is* a body. English approximates this pattern when it speaks of "somebody," "anybody," or "if a body meet a body coming through the rye." This is an aspective view of one seen also as holistic.

Käsemann correctly sees that Paul, who makes much of *sōma,* does not use *sōma* for the modern idea of person as personality in the sense of "individuality." In the anthropology of classical Greece, *sōma* stood for limitation and individuation, but in Paul it stands for the possibility of communication and relationship.[8]

A most exciting usage for "body" is its corporate use for the church, the body of Christ. This will be studied in detail in Chapter 3, where the polarity of individuality and corporeity is reviewed. Paul especially uses the body as the model for "a vast solidarity of historical existence" which he terms the "body of sin" (Rom. 6:6) or "body of death" (Rom. 7:24), and for the "body of Christ" (I Cor. 10:16, and *passim*) into which one is brought in salvation.[9] Paul's doctrine is not a "body of Christians" but "the body of Christ." [10] This is the thought behind the words of Jesus instituting the Lord's Supper, "This is my body," referring not only to the body given up at Golgotha but also to the body created by him, the church, the body of Christ (I Cor. 10:16 f.). It was this "body" which the Corinthians were not discerning (I Cor. 11:29). Through their failure to wait for some of their brethren as they ate what they thought was the Lord's Supper they reduced it to their own supper (I Cor. 11:20 f.).

In this corporate use of "body," individuality is not sacrificed. "Body" does not on the one hand imply a partitive idea, reducing man to a body-soul dichotomy, nor does it imply absorption into the divine or into the church with the loss of individual, personal identity. Whether in "the body of sin" or in "the body of Christ," individuality remains in a tension with solidarity.

The New Testament knows of no disembodied soul or spirit. Wherever envisioned, in this life or the next, man is always in a body. As to the next life, the Biblical doctrine is resurrection, not immortality of the soul.[11] The precise nature of the resurrected body is not spelled out, but two things are affirmed: its continuity with the present body and its transformation (I Cor. 15:35–58). As between seed sown and the new life produced there is both continuity and discontinuity, so between the body sown (birth or death?) and the body raised. For our purpose, it is important to note that body belongs essentially to what man is. It is not a tomb or prison for the soul. It is not a part that can be shed. Man is a body, in creation, in sin, in redemption, in life beyond death. *Sōma* stands for the whole person considered from the standpoint of his external, physical existence; and, when contrasted with *sarx, sōma* stands for the whole man in solidarity with creation but as made for God, while *sarx* stands for his distance from God.[12]

Sarx. Like *psychē* and *sōma, sarx* can be used for the whole man, seen in his natural state, in his weakness, or in his hostility to God. It is not so much that man *has* flesh as that he *is* flesh or may be flesh. This term, found about 140 times in the New Testament, is used with varying connotation, and it may describe man aspectively or holistically. Better stated, it may designate the whole man from a given perspective, that of his literal flesh or "ethically" from the perspective of his distance from God. Sometimes *sarx* is used with no special connotation, except to refer to a man or mankind.

The most elementary use of *sarx* is for the visible substance of the body, "the whole person, considered from the point of view of his external, physical existence."[13] When it is said that one's flesh "did not see corruption" (Acts 2:31), the obvious reference is to literal flesh. In this sense it may refer to the flesh of man or the lower animals, birds, and fish (I Cor. 15:39; Phil. 1:22, 24; I Tim. 3:16; Heb. 5:7; I John 4:2; II John 7; Rev. 17:16; 19:18, 21). Sometimes *sarx* refers to "fleshly" or natural lineage, as when Paul refers to his kinsmen according to flesh (Rom. 9:3).

"Flesh" or "flesh and blood" may serve simply for the whole man or mankind. When Paul did not confer with "flesh and blood" (Gal. 1:16), he meant that he did not talk with people. When he says that "no human being" (RSV) shall be justified out of the works of the law (Rom. 3:20), he uses the word *sarx*. In I Cor. 1:29 he likewise uses *sarx* for saying that "no human being" may boast before God. When Paul said that upon reaching Troas, "our flesh got no rest" (II Cor. 7:5) he did not mean that he was physically tired, but that his anxiety over the problems in Corinth were not relieved, since Titus was not there as he had hoped. By "our flesh" he means "I."

Probably *sarx* stands for man in Matt. 16:17: "Flesh and blood has not revealed this to you." Clearly in Matt. 24:22, "no flesh" means "no human being," just as in Luke 3:6 "all flesh" means all people who are to see God's salvation. The discourse in John, ch. 6, is most instructive, where there is interchange between "my flesh" (John 6:51–56) and "me" (John 6:57). To "eat" Christ's flesh is to "eat" him. Clearly then, "flesh" can designate the whole person simply as person, or it can designate the whole man in his weakness or distance from God. In no case is *sarx* used in a dichotomous or partitive sense or with the implication that flesh as material is evil.

The "ethical" use of the term "flesh" is both prominent and significant in the New Testament. By "ethical" is meant non-literal, man in his moral or ethical weakness or man apart from God. In this usage, "flesh" may refer to any aspect of man or to man in his entirety. "Flesh" thus used may refer to emotions or will as well as to appetite. It has no special reference to the body as such or to its sensual nature. In this usage, "flesh" stands in contrast to "spirit." The "fleshly" man is one apart from redemption; the "spiritual" man is man under redemption. When Paul writes, "You are not in the flesh, you are in the Spirit, if the Spirit of God really dwells in you" (Rom. 8:9), he is not suggesting that the Roman Christians are ghosts or disembodied spirits. They were in the literal flesh, else Paul would not be sending them a letter written with ink on papyrus or parchment. Paul is not suggesting that they were physically any less in the flesh than any pagan, but he is using the term ethically. They are no longer living of themselves, apart from the Spirit of God.

Paul can look back upon his preconversion life as a time when "we were living in the flesh" (Rom. 7:5). Surely he was yet living in the literal flesh. Contextual evidence compels us to understand his use of "flesh" here as nonliteral. When he says, "Nothing good dwells within me, that is, in my flesh," he does not restrict the reference to the literal flesh. He means himself apart from God, apart from redemption. To be "carnal" (*sarki-*

kos) is not necessarily to be sensuous. In fact, one of Paul's illustrations in context has to do with coveting (Rom. 7:7 f.). Most significant is his catalog of "the works of the flesh" (Gal. 5:19). Of the fifteen examples listed, only five are sensual (fornication, impurity, licentiousness, drunkenness, carousing), while ten are non-sensual or what we term "sins of the spirit" (idolatry, sorcery, enmity, strife, jealousy, anger, selfishness, dissension, party spirit or factionalism, envy).

So, jealousy and envy are as "carnal" as are fornication and drunkenness. There is here no Gnostic despising of the literal flesh. The flesh as such is not evil. That "the Word became flesh" (John 1:14) is itself conclusive evidence that flesh as such is not evil. Neither is there a dichotomy implied. The whole man, in every aspect of his selfhood, may be "flesh" or "spirit." The phrase "according to flesh" (*kata sarka*) may denote only one's natural state, as "my kinsmen according to flesh" (Rom. 9:3), but usually it contrasts with "according to spirit," to show one's distance from God. One may "walk" according to flesh or spirit (Rom. 8:4). Obviously the reference is not to one's physical walking but to one's kind of existence or manner of living. One may "purpose" according to flesh (II Cor. 1:17), "know" according to flesh (II Cor. 5:16), "war" according to flesh (II Cor. 10:3), "live" according to flesh (Rom. 8:13), "judge" according to flesh (John 8:15), or "have one's being" according to flesh (Rom. 8:5).

When Paul declares that he no longer regards Christ or any man "according to flesh" (II Cor. 5:16), he does not imply indifference to their bodily or historical existence, but he means that he no longer regards Christ or any man "from a human point of view," i.e., through the eyes of an unregenerate man. Thus acts of reason, of will, or feeling may be "flesh" or "carnal." The phrase "in flesh," as seen above, may refer to one's literal bodily existence (II Cor. 10:3; Gal. 2:20) or to one's distance from God (Rom. 7:5; 8:9). Only context can tell.

When Jesus said to Nicodemus, "That which is born of flesh is flesh, and that which is born of the Spirit is spirit" (John 3:6), he may have intended to contrast the natural, physical birth with one from above. Probably, however, "flesh" here refers to the whole religious striving of Nicodemus. His earnest effort to attain eternal life through observance of the law was his own human effort, however honest and well-meaning. It was not that he needed to try harder, for life was not to be found down that road of human effort. That was "flesh." Eternal life is a gift to be received from God. Nicodemus was "carnal" or walking according to "flesh," but there is not a hint that his problem was sensual. This agrees with Rom., ch. 8, where those who walk according to flesh are those who seek salvation through keeping the law whereas those who walk according to the Spirit are those who receive in faith God's gracious gift of life (Rom. 8:2–17).

Those who try to complete their religious pilgrimage in the "flesh" (Gal. 3:3) are not those tempted to sensual passions but those who trust in circumcision and other works of the law. Zeal for the law and pride in family and personal virtues and achievements are alike "flesh" (Phil. 3:3–7). The self-reliant attitude of the man who trusts in his own strength and performance is the one who is oriented by "flesh" and who lives out of "flesh." [14] Nicodemus and the Pharisaic Saul of Tarsus were both living "according to flesh," not in sensuality but in the pride of their own achievements. This "mind of the flesh" is unconsciously or unintentionally suicidal (Rom. 8:6), for it is self-destruction in the very act of seeking salvation. It is "hostile to God" (Rom. 8:7), even if unintentionally so, for it seeks salvation out of one's own resources. This is to put "confidence in the flesh" (Phil. 3:3), i.e., in oneself.

Although used in at least a half dozen ways in the New Testament, *sarx* is not used in a dichotomous way, nor is it used to imply that flesh as such is evil. It may see man aspectively, from the standpoint of his weakness or distance from God, but it is the whole man who is thus seen. "Worldliness," with no special reference to sensuousness, comes close to being the modern equivalent.

Pneuma. The term *pneuma* has figured prominently in dichotomous or trichotomous views of man, body-spirit, flesh-spirit, or body-soul-spirit. There are traces of such anthropological language in the New Testament, as in I Thess. 5:23, "May your spirit and soul and body be kept sound and blameless at the coming of our Lord Jesus Christ." As seen above, this may best be understood as the traditional language of liturgy and as not to be pressed for Pauline anthropology. At least there is little if any supporting evidence for a serious trichotomous scheme in Paul's writings, and there is much evidence to the contrary.

Like *psychē, sōma,* and *sarx, pneuma* can be used for the whole man, seen from a given perspective. Of course the term is used in a wide variety of ways, from a designation of the wind to the Spirit of God (John 3:8). Moulton and Geden require almost five full pages to list the occurrences of *pneuma* in its various meanings.[15] Our concern here is for its implications for the nature of man.

Just as *sarx* is often used to characterize the whole man in his distance from God, so *pneuma* is often used to characterize man in his relationship with God. Bultmann sums it up well: "Man does not consist of two parts, much less of three; nor are *psychē* and *pneuma* special faculties or principles (within the *sōma*) of a mental life higher than his animal life. Rather, man is a living unity." [16] *Pneuma* can be used in place of a personal pronoun, for the whole person. When Paul writes, "for they refreshed my spirit as well as yours" (I Cor. 16:18), he means they refreshed "me and you." Benedictions that evoke God's blessings upon "your spirit" mean "upon you" (Gal. 6:18; Phil. 4:23; Philemon, v. 25). Paul writes that when he did not find Titus at Troas he found no rest, saying first "my spirit" (II Cor. 2:13) and then "our flesh" (II Cor. 7:5). In each case he means that his anxiety was unrelieved. The whole man was involved, not just a "lower" or "higher" part. When Stephen prays, "Lord Jesus, receive my spirit," he means "receive me" (Acts 7:59).

Never in Scripture is man envisoned as a disembodied spirit. At the transfiguration of Jesus, Moses and Elijah appear as recognizable persons, for whom Peter wanted to build "booths" (Mark 9:5). The rich man, Lazarus, and Abraham are pictured in bodily form in Luke, ch. 16, the rich man with a parched tongue and the other two in a banquet setting. Admittedly these pictures are not to be pressed, but however taken, they at least know nothing of Orphic or Platonic "immortal souls" or disembodied spirits. Man is always somatic. He may be "flesh" or "spirit," i.e., cut off from meaningful relationship with God or in a redemptive relationship.

Paul makes a sharp distinction between the "spiritual" (*pneumatikos*) man and one described as "carnal" (*sarkikos* or *sarkinos*) or "unspiritual" (*psychikos*). "Spiritual" persons are ones who have received "the Spirit which is from God" (I Cor. 2:12). They are those "who possess the Spirit" and to whom "spiritual truths" can be imparted (I Cor. 2:13). By contrast, the "worldly" (*psychikoi*) are those not having the Spirit (Jude, v. 19). Evidence that one is not "spiritual" comes not alone from sensuality but especially from the presence in a life of such things as "jealousy and strife" (I Cor. 3:3). The "worldly" or those "of the flesh" walk like ordinary men, according to men and not according to God's Spirit. One can know that he is not "in the flesh" but "in the Spirit" if the Spirit of God or Christ dwells in him (Rom. 8:9–11).

Paul's clearest indication of what "spirituality" is may be found in Gal. 5:22, where the fruit of the Spirit is characterized as "love, joy, peace, patience, kindness, goodness, faithfulness, gentleness, self-control." This kind of existence is contrasted with "the flesh" (Gal. 5:24) in a context where the pride and self-confidence of legalism is the chief threat to true spirituality. In this usage "flesh" and "spirit" are not to be taken as the material and nonmaterial but as the total man alone or with God. Each sees the total man aspectively and holistically.

PRACTICAL IMPLICATIONS

How man is understood, partitively or aspectively, dichotomous or holistic, makes tremendous difference. This holds for salvation, for ministry, and even for ecology. Recovery of the Biblical understanding of man as aspective but holistic opens the way to

a richer understanding of salvation, a heavier responsibility in
ministry to man, and even a more responsible care for God's
good earth, the larger "body" or "house" ("ecology" is from
oikos, "house") in which we live.

Salvation is not the reduction of life through asceticism or
otherwise. It does not mean the rejection of the body. Neither
does it mean the surrender of intelligence or freedom of will.
Jesus came to give life in abundance (John 10:10), not to shrink
it. Salvation is not becoming an ascetic fragment through rejection of the body, nor is it becoming an angel or a ghost. It is to
become a human being, nothing more and nothing less. It is to
come into such relationship with God that one is freed from all
such destructive forces as greed, lust, envy, jealousy, fear, prejudice, and hate. It is to be cleansed and renewed. It is to be given
new direction and new resources for life. It is to come alive!
It is to become a true human being in all the aspects of a unitary
or holistic existence.

How man is understood also affects one's understanding of
ministry. The long and regrettable debate over a "personal" or
"social" gospel is uninformed. It misses the Biblical doctrine of
man as holistic in his aspective complexity. Jesus was concerned
with the whole man, as were the great prophets of Israel before
him. Jesus fed the hungry, healed the sick, forgave sinners, accepted the rejects of society, and responded to human need at
every level and expression (cf. Luke 4:18 ff.; 7:22 ff.). He
offered fulfillment, not emptiness. He came to make the whole
man sound or whole (John 7:23). He knew of no conflict between
a personal and a social gospel. He brought the individual to God,
into a new relationship with the community, and into a new
understanding of the individual's own identity. Ministry is to be
as wide as humanity (to all people) and as inclusive as the
total complexity of man.

Of the many factors contributing to our ecological crisis one
is traceable to Orphic or Platonic corruption of our thought.
A dichotomy between matter and spirit is not only anti-Biblical
but ecologically fatal. If philosophy or religion teaches us to
despise the material, counting it worthless or even evil, the next

step is to neglect it, abuse it, deplete it, pollute it. It is a sin against God to thus despise what he has created, and it is a stupid act of self-destruction so to do. A holistic understanding of man is complemented by a holistic view of the larger "house" that God has made for us.

PARTITIVE VIEWS OF SELFHOOD

Having surveyed some of the Biblical evidence for man's aspective yet holistic nature, we could end the chapter here. Unfortunately, however, Biblical perspective has often been obscured by other views, ancient and modern. Some of these views impinged upon pre-Christian Judaism and some of them have strongly affected the Christian community from its earliest days. Although a tedious task and actually outside the limits of Biblical theology, a survey now of some competing views may serve to expose both correspondence and variance between Biblical and other perspectives. For this vast world of thought I must rely heavily on the expertise of others, as indicated.

The so-called "Greek" view of man, with its dualism of soul and body, made some impact upon late Judaism, as e.g., in the Jewish apocryphal book The Wisdom of Solomon, and it had extensive influence upon the Christian movement, especially as the movement became more Gentile and less Jewish in character. "Greek" is a somewhat misleading term, for not all Greek thought was dualistic and this dualism entered Greek thought from outside influences, being chiefly adapted from the Thracian worship of Dionysus as it entered Greece through Orphism.

Homer. The earliest literary evidence for Greek understanding of man is found in Homer's *Iliad* and *Odyssey*. These works are themselves not absolutely consistent, for they undoubtedly are based upon a long epic tradition, and they seem to reflect, especially in rituals that had outlived the theology behind them, older views that do not fully agree with Homer's own. Homer had some concept of life after death, but his chief interest was in man's present, bodily life. He had little interest in the "soul" once it was separated from the body. Homer preserved something of an older view that the "shade of the deceased hovered around the tomb" until the body disintegrated, but his "more normal view was that the soul is linked with the final breath, given up in death." [17] That which survives death is *psychē,* soul or shade. This life after death was "not far from non-existent." [18] Souls or shades in Hades possessed neither strength nor consciousness and in their "unconscious half-life" were of little or no interest to Homer.[19] His interest was in the joyous, vigorous life in the light of the sun, not in the empty existence of souls in Hades.[20]

Homer neither aspired to the shadowy existence of souls in Hades nor feared such souls. "Man in Homer has liberated himself from the fear of the dead but not from the fear of death." [21] No cult of the dead is required, for powerless "shades" do not have to be propitiated or worshiped. It is the emptiness of meaning for souls in Hades which is dreaded.

According to Erwin Rohde, Homer saw human beings as existing twice over: "once as an outward and visible shape, and again as an invisible 'image' which only gains its freedom in death. This, and nothing else, is the psyche." [22] Death was no friend to Homer. Never would he have accepted the proposition, "Who knows then whether Life be not Death, and what we here call Death be called Life there below?" He has Achilles say to Odysseus in Hades, "Do not try to explain away death to me." Death is the hated enemy which ends life in the sunlight.

For Homer, death did not completely end one's existence, for the *psychē* did go into Hades. The *psychē* was not thought of as "spirit" opposed to body.[23] The corpse falls to pieces, and the *psychē* is then without feeling, will, or thought. It is only in life, in the union of psyche and body, that one is fully man. For a few only, special favorites of the gods, was there escape from death and Hades, through translation to the "Elysian plain" at the end or edge of the world, a land where "there falls not rain, nor hail, nor snow" and where the gods live (*Odyssey,* IV). Only these become "immortal." To Homer, "immortal" and "god" are interchangeable terms, applied to those whose psyche is never separated from the body.[24]

Orphic Mysteries. In the sixth century B.C. something significant entered into Greek thought, opening up a new understanding of man's nature and destiny. This innovation came through Orphism, which in turn drew its inspiration from the Thracian worship of Dionysus. The new understanding was that man is a dualism of body and immortal soul, the soul being a divine creation with greater freedom and fulfillment outside the body than within it.

The god known to the Greeks as "Dionysus" was known in Thracia by various names, including "Zagreus," "Sabos," and "Sabazios." The Thracian cult held torchlight festivals on mountaintops or slopes in the darkness of night, accompanied by the thunderous music of bronze cymbals, kettledrums, and flutes and wild dancing and shrill crying. The frantic whirling in circular dances continued until the dancers, mostly women, carrying snakes sacred to Sabazios, reached a "sacred frenzy" and then fell upon some beast selected as their victim, tearing him apart and devouring the raw flesh.[25] By means of this self-induced mania, the worshipers achieved some sense of a "spirituality" that broke through physical barriers.

In this "sacred madness" the "soul" seemed to leave the body to enter into union with the god. This union with their god (*entheos*) was their "enthusiasm" or god-intoxication. This state of ecstasy (*ekstasis*), a standing out of oneself, was the chief object of the cult. From this sense of a soul freed from the body during the ecstatic experience came the further idea of a continuing, independent existence of the soul after the death of the body, i.e., the idea of a divine and immortal soul.[26] With this view, death lost its threat and was seen as entrance into the higher life of the soul.

Orphism built upon the myth of Dionysus (also called Zagreus), son of Zeus and Persephone. According to the myth, the wicked Titans tricked Dionysus, tore his body to pieces, and devoured him. Athena rescued the heart and took it to Zeus, who swallowed it. From Zeus came a new Dionysus (Zagreus). In an extended form of the legend, Zeus killed the Titans with lightning and from their ashes sprang the race of men who combined good from Dionysus and evil from the Titans. The Titanic element came to represent the body and the Dionysiac element the soul. From this is the idea of the freeing of the Dionysiac element (the soul) from the Titanic (the body) so that the soul might return to its divine origin.

From this background four far-reaching ideas penetrated Greek thought, with implications subsequently for the understanding of man throughout the Western world: (1) the body as the prison house for the soul, (2) the soul as fallen and requiring redemption, (3) transmigration of souls, and (4) the conception of disincarnate or disembodied immortality.[27]

Plato is often quoted as saying *"Sōma sēma"* ("The body is a tomb"). Actually, the saying goes back to Orphism, a major influence upon Plato. Literally the Greek words are "Body sign," presumably meaning that the visible body is but the outward sign for the true self, the soul. This is the basic dualism behind much philosophy and religion from Orphism on. Body and soul are seen as not only separate but hostile to one another. To this day much popular religion and some that appears to be sophisticated (much of it passing as "Christian"), builds upon this Orphic dualism, probably in turn derived from the wild orgies of Dionysus.

With the view that the soul, the true self, is imprisoned within the body is the view that it must be purified from bodily defilement. This was first sought through ritual practice and later through moral endeavor. In gnosticism, deliverance of soul from body came primarily through a special knowledge, although ritual and ascetic practices had their place.

The idea of transmigration of souls grew out of the belief that the soul was so deeply imprisoned in the body that more than one lifetime was required for its deliverance. The soul's tragedy was that it was caught in the "wheel of nature" (*kyklos tēs geneseōs*), a cycle of birth-death-rebirth. The fortunate eventually broke out of this cycle to return to their true element, but the rest were doomed to repeat the cycle endlessly.

The idea of human destiny in terms of disincarnate immortality is far removed from Homer. To Homer nothing could be

less desired than a *psyche* in Hades, a shade of selfhood separated from the body. To Orphism the ultimate was the soul
freed from its bodily prison for an unencumbered life. Homer
rejoiced in a vigorous, bodily life in the sunshine. Orphism
sought escape from bodily existence. Death was the hateful enemy to Homer but friendly release for Orphism. Homer was
oriented to the present, Orphism to the future. Through Pythagoras, Plato, and others, views of Orphism were worked out in
ways that yet impinge upon (or plague) us.

Pythagoras. The philosophy of Pythagoras of Samos (d. 497
B.C.) was a practical one, concerned to understand "the nature of
man" and show him "the way and purpose of his living." [28] Pythagoras' doctrine of the soul was the center of his teaching. He
believed that man's soul had been cast down from divine heights
and as a punishment confined to the body. He saw no kinship
between body and soul. The air was filled with souls, and any
soul could dwell in any body. When separated from the body by
death, the soul was required to spend some time in Hades to be
purged before it could return to the upper world. A soul on
earth had to find residence in a body, and it could inhabit the
body of man or beast. With this was the idea of reincarnation,
the soul moving up or down in the scale, depending upon its behavior. Early Pythagoreans were ascetic, with a low view of the
body. Their vegetarianism was traceable both to asceticism and
the view that the body of an animal might be the dwelling of a
soul, possibly of a deceased relative or friend.

Platonic Dualism. The view that man is constituted of two
parts, i.e., is dualistic or dichotomous (in some cases trichotomous or polychotomous), thus has its roots deep in the ancient
world. Probably the deepest roots are in pre-Christian Greek
philosophy, expressed in particular in the thought of Plato and
his followers. Plato more than any other was responsible for
popularizing the idea of an immortal soul. His teacher, Socrates,
had little interest in an assurance about life after death and
neither did the masses of Greeks before Plato.

Plato (427?–347 B.C.), drawing heavily upon Orphism, saw
man as constituted of soul (*psyche*) and body (*soma*)—an un-

happy partnership in life, happily dissolved by death. By soul (*psychē*) he meant fundamentally "reason" (*nous*), seeing the immaterial in man to be *nous*. The soul itself Plato saw as tripartite: the immortal part being pure reason, the spirited aspect being the nobler impulses of the heart (anger, love of power, ambition), and the appetitive aspect being the lower appetites and passions situated in the liver.[29] He saw the real self as the soul, the body being its temporary tomb or prison. This is epitomized in the borrowed pun, "*Sōma sēma*," meaning that the body (*sōma*) is but a sign (*sēma*) for selfhood. In his description of the death of Socrates (*Phaedo*), Plato has Socrates drive home the point that soul is "soul and body is body, and that neither is the other." [30] Death is seen as the separation of body and soul. Death, then, was the instrument of salvation, for salvation consisted of release from the body. The victory of soul over body began with ascetic discipline and rites, and the battle could continue through successive reincarnations before the soul was permanently freed from its prison or tomb, the body.

In the *Phaedo* and in the *Phaedrus* (245D-E) the soul is seen as a sempiternal entity, i.e., having preexistence and postexistence. There is some contrary evidence in the *Philebus* (30C), where the suggestion is made that the individual soul may be derived from the soul of the universe, and in the *Laws* (X, 899C), where it is said that the soul is the first thing to become. It is not clear whether Plato's view changed toward the latter part of his life or that his reference to the genesis of the soul may only imply "a relation of sempiternal subordination between the soul and the Deity."[31] At least, Plato represented Socrates as holding to both the preexistence and postexistence of the soul. Socrates had little trouble convincing his hearers of the preexistence of the soul but more trouble convincing them that the soul survived death. For people today in the Western world, the doctrine of creation (Semitic and not Greek) precludes or seriously modifies the idea of preexistence; for them the burden falls upon the belief in survival after death.

Another unresolved tension in the view of Plato relates to his seemingly personalist conception of immortality (a full person and not just reason) and his view that death is a dissolution of soul and body, for it would seem that the personalist conception of immortality would call for the transformation of the whole man (resurrection) and not dissolution.[32] The term "soul" (*psychē*) is used in various ways, and Plato's conception of it seems to be "under the pull of divergent forces, the one trying to reduce it to pure reason, the other trying to keep it something personal." [33] That the *psychē* was "reason" (*nous*) was his dominant view.

Plato saw the soul (as *nous,* or "reason") as the essential self. The soul was encumbered by the body, which constantly distracted it from its proper business, i.e., to think and to gain knowledge. But this view was not fully correlated with yet another thesis, that the soul gives life to the body and directs its activities.[34] How may the soul direct the body and yet be distracted by it?

In any event, Plato influenced many in the direction of a dualistic or dichotomous view of man and also toward the despising of the body. Christians who hold to a body-soul dichotomy and who incline to ascetic denial of the body owe more to Plato than to the Bible.

Aristotle. Plato's most famous student, Aristotle, broke with his teacher at some significant points. He rejected as unsatisfactory Plato's unresolved dualism between form and matter. He found forms to be inherent in matter, immanent and not transcendent. There is no form without matter. True being he found to be the essence that unfolds in phenomena themselves. Rejecting Plato's universals, Aristotle found that the universal is real only in the particular. Although he found matter and form to be inseparable, he did find them to be distinguishable, the distinction being that of potentiality and actuality. Form is true being. Form is the self-realization of matter in its actualization. In other words, being comes to existence as the forms which are already in matter come to realization in terms of their ends or purposes.[35] Although the Aristotelian understanding of man is not to be equated with the Hebrew-Christian view, its view of man's nature as unitary is more compatible with the Biblical view than is Platonic dualism, which unfortunately has had the greater influence on Christian thinking.

Gnostic Dualism. The deepest thrust of a metaphysical dualism into the Christian world probably came with what is known as gnosticism. The basic tenet of gnosticism was that matter is evil and that only spirit is good. The material was not seen as "fallen" but as originally and inherently evil. In some systems it was attributed to an inferior and evil creator god. Man was seen as essentially soul or spirit, unfortunately fallen into a body, or as essentially spirit encased in a soul and this in turn encased in a body.[36] Salvation was seen as release from the body through ascetic practice and certain mystical rites directed to the gaining of *gnōsis,* saving knowledge. This once open and vigorous movement within Christendom lives on in ascetic practices (celibacy, food laws, etc.), in all denial of the material world and the "material" side of man's nature, and in the popular belief in an "immortal soul" as some entity somewhere within the body.

Too little is known about the origin and early development of "gnosticism" to allow for dogmatic statements. It is not known for certain whether the movement was pre-Christian or not.[37] It is not known whether it arose in paganism, Judaism, or Christianity. It does not necessarily follow that there was a monolithic gnosticism at the first. Probably there were first tendencies, varied in expression from community to community, and that there gradually developed the forms of gnosticism which emerge with clarity during the second century of the Christian era. Whatever its origin and precise early forms, it went far in shaping (or distorting) the Christian doctrine of man. Gnosticism is not dead; of its views and values much lives on in the church today.

Robert M. Grant observes that the term is used today to indicate a constellation of speculative religious phenomena found in the second century and later encountered from Gaul in the West to Iran in the East.[38] He describes them thus:

These phenomena include beliefs in the innate immortality of a divine spark, differentiated from both body and soul; the neces-

sity for the escape of this element to its source, an unknown
God; the control of the visible universe by evil spirits; and the
bringing of knowledge (*gnōsis*) about the unknown god and
the divine element by a redeemer who descends to earth and
returns alone, having effected redemption by providing this
knowledge to those who "by origin" are related to him.[39]

He writes, "Gnostics knew that they were originally spiritual
beings who have come to live in souls and bodies; they once
dwelt in the spiritual world above but have been made to fall
into the world of sense and sin." [40]

Robert McL. Wilson concurs in the recognition of the elusive-
ness of Gnostic origins and early development and offers this
distinction: "By Gnosticism we mean the specifically Christian
heresy of the second century A.D., by Gnosis, in a broader sense,
the whole complex of ideas belonging to the Gnostic movement
and related trends of thought." [41] He finds that particular motifs
and concepts present in gnosticism can be traced back into the
pre-Christian period, whether or not these motifs can themselves
be called Gnostic until their appearance in the later developed
Gnostic systems.[42] He sees gnosticism as fundamentally syncre-
tistic, drawing elements from diverse cultures, but he agrees
with Bultmann that the essence of gnosticism is not in the
syncretism but in its new understanding of man and the world.[43]

In many Gnostic systems three classes of men were recognized:
spiritual (*pneumatikos*), psychics (*psychikos*), and carnal (*sarkikos*). The "spiritual" were by nature and origin saved; the
"psychics" had the latent capacity for gnosis, so could possibly
be saved; and the "carnal" ("earthly" or "material") were hope-
lessly lost.[44] Most important for our study is the Gnostic's dualistic understanding of man as soul and body. More carefully
stated, the Gnostic saw man as spirit enveloped in a soul which
in turn was enveloped in a body.

The ground for this view was prepared in Greek philosophy
and religion. The Hellenistic world thought of the universe as a
system of concentric spheres rising above and around the earth,
each ruled by an astral angel or minor divinity and in some way
controlling human destiny.[45] Plato distinguished between the

ideal world and that perceptible to the senses, some men belonging to the ideal world above the spheres, where God dwelt.[46]
The Stoics held that the soul was a spark of the divine fire en-
closed in matter from which it sought release through ascetic
practice and cleansing from fleshly lusts, magic knowledge of
the names of ruling powers and of passwords, or by mystic
vision and enlightenment.[47] It was an easy step from this to the
Gnostic understanding of man, of the world, and of salvation,
whatever the catalyst or immediate situation for the rise of
Christian gnosticism, whether Hellenistic philosophy, Oriental
religion (chiefly Iranian), heterodox Judaism (Grant proposes
disappointed Jewish apocalypticism),[48] or something within
Christianity itself.

Gnosticism probably came close to prevailing in the second
and third centuries but was finally repudiated by the church as a
whole. It has lived on incognito despite its inadequate answer to
the problems of human existence, its notion that man is essentially
or entirely "spiritual" with a denial of the bodily and historical
side of his existence and with its emphasis upon salvation as
escape from man's bodily and historical existence.[49] Gnosticism's
outlook included a radical acosmism, repudiation of this world and
man's existence in it; and in this it contradicts the Biblical view
that God created the world and that he created man in his bodily,
historical existence. The Gnostic view that the world will return
to its primordial chaos contradicts the Biblical view that man is to
continue God's work of triumph over chaos in having dominion
over the works of his hands.[50] In brief, gnosticism is world-deny-
ing; Christianity is world-affirming.

Above all, gnosticism failed precisely where it was most
concerned to succeed, in man's understanding of himself and in
the gaining of his authentic existence. Its concern was with knowledge (gnōsis), not just any knowledge but self-knowledge. The
Gnostic wanted to know himself, to know himself in terms of his
kinship to the divine, seeing himself as a "spark" of the divine
and longing to return to the world of pure spirit. But the Gnostic's self-knowledge was woefully inadequate. He rightly saw
himself as kin to God, but he wrongly denied the creaturely side

of his existence, including the bodily and historical. He denied the "polarity" of his existence: created in the image of God, in the image of God but not God; created, an authentic creature and more.

In their quest for self-understanding, freedom, and fulfillment, the Gnostics succumbed to partition or fragmentizing in the place of wholeness. They sought freedom through escape. They saw salvation in terms of reduction of selfhood and life. Jesus taught salvation in terms of the abundance of life, its enlargement and not its reduction.

THE BODY-MIND RELATIONSHIP

Philosophy and science, as well as religion, have long been concerned with the question of the relationship between body and mind. That question as such is not the object of this chapter, but it is our concern to see that there are no compelling understandings of the body-mind relationship that preclude the Biblical, aspective-holistic nature of man.

Probably the most ancient and persistent dichotomous view of man is that which sees him as body and mind or body and soul. There has never been agreement at this point. Aristotle (384–322 B.C.) thought of man in terms of "compositionism," man as "a single integral substance" rather than two.[51] He saw mind and body as complementing one another in closest union and as not having separate existence in living persons. Body and soul or matter and form went together, the soul giving life, unity, and purpose to the body.[52] The Stoics had a monistic view, holding that the human soul was but a fragment from the world soul, a spark from the divine or cosmic flame to which periodically it would return.

Descartes (1596–1650) saw mind and body as distinct entities, completely separate from one another except for one elusive point of contact which he likened to the relationship between a horse and its rider.[53] Closer to the thought of Plato, this is a rejection of Aristotle's view of the unity of personality, for it sees body as a machinelike structure separate from mind. Descartes did not really explain the complex interactions between body and mind.

Yet another approach to the understanding of man's nature is that of George Berkeley (1685–1753). He contended that all material objects were simply projections of the mind. Even the classroom and students are but such projections, existing only in the mind of the professor (ultimately in the mind of God). When a friend, after hurting his foot on a rock, protested that the foot and the rock were real, Berkeley could argue that the foot and the rock existed only because they were in the mind of God. Thus the "material" world about us exists only in the mind. He did not deny the reality of the world but rather its materiality. This is a form of monism, the doctrine that there is only one kind of ultimate reality. He denied that things have "an absolute existence distinct from being perceived by God and exterior to *all* minds." [54]

The idea heard today in some Christian circles that the dead live on only as a memory in the mind of God, though not the same, sounds more like the above than the New Testament.

A current form of monism is that which recognizes the existence of body but not mind, seeing thought as simply the function of a brain and nervous system or "the chemico-electrical activity of billions of brain cells discharging in incredibly complex patterns throughout the cortex and brain stem." [55] This may serve as a scientific description of certain processes, but it does not explain thought, feeling, choosing, or anything else of ultimate concern to us. It does not explain what triggers the opening or closing of a hand. It only picks up the process at a certain point without explaining how I can "will" to open or close my hand.

Those who resist "monism" in favor of a "dualism" which sees body and mind as two things rather than one are not in agreement among themselves as to the pattern of this dualism. J. O. Wisdom sums up the options thus:

The well-known theories about the possible relations between them [mind and body] can be divided into the following: (1) the mind acts on the body and the body acts on the mind (Interaction or Interactionist Dualism); (2) occurrences in the mind are paralleled by occurrences in the body or *vice versa*, without Interaction (Parallelism or Parallelistic Dualism); (3) the mind is "reducible to" the body (Epiphenomenalism or Materialistic Monism); (4) the body is "reducible to" the mind (Idealism or Idealistic Monism); and (5) the mind and body are "reducible to" a third "stuff" (Neutral Monism).[56]

That there is some kind of relationship between "mind" and "body," that each has some kind of control over the other, and that each has some kind of independence of the other—these seem to be inescapable conclusions, but there yet remains much mystery along with increasing light. No case can be made for "disembodied minds" or for living bodies without minds,[57] but neither can we offer any fully satisfactory answer as to their relationship. That there is some kind of connection between mind and brain is apparent, but precisely what that connection is remains in part a mystery. Von Bonin finds it impossible to answer the simple question as to how the brain steers motor mechanisms, e.g., the muscles: "Again, we must confess to our ignorance as to the exact way in which that happens. We know that always there is first an intention to do something, and then the actual execution follows." [58]

That there is a physical basis and a physiological substructure of personhood, including mind, is increasingly substantiated by science, and it is congenial to the Hebrew view of man as holistic in nature. Eric C. Rust observes:

More and more we are made aware of the interrelationship of a body chemistry and our personal characteristics, of the intimate bond between the brain and our mental activity, of the implications of our genetic structure for our personal development.[59]

Rust rejects the view that the glands of the body and their hormones *determine* certain aspects of the personality, but he recognizes that they provide a chemical base within which the personality and its traits have to operate.[60]

But to Rust, more primal than our body chemistry is the genetic structure which we inherit.[61] Every living cell of the human body, except the seed cells, possesses in its nucleus forty-eight paired chromosomes, twenty-four from each parent, and these highly complex organic molecules are "coded" by genes. These DNA (desoxyribonucleic acid) molecules, coded by the genes, "carry not only our physical traits but also our behavioristic ones." [62] Thus we carry our heredity in every cell of our body, and this means "many personal characteristics which seem bound up with our mental and spiritual life are inherited by and bound up with a physiological structure which has a chemical base." [63]

The debate continues about the relationship between mind and brain. Epiphenomenalism is a materialistic view which sees mind as emerging from matter and thus as derivative from its material base and materialistically determined. Acknowledging that mind has emerged from matter, Rust holds that "this by no means supports the idea that mind is a refined form of the material order, a reflection of its processes." [64] He also sees that mind is always associated with a physical and physiological base but that this "does not imply that matter *determines* the functioning of mind even though it provides the condition in which mind emerges." [65] To be rejected is the naturalism which understands mind simply as a closed system of cause and effect in a physical chain which allows no place for a nonphysical agent.[66] Mind is "an aspect of personal being which cannot be reduced to the level of cerebral, physiological, or material structures." [67] Rust sums up the matter thus:

> The picture of man which is being developed is neither a radically dualistic one nor a monistic one, neither materialistic nor idealistic. That mind should emerge creatively within the physiochemical and biological levels is at least a reminder that the physical and physiological are not inimical to the mental, and we have seen enough reason at the scientific level to support the separate status of mind.[68]

Man has a mind and has a brain, but man is a person in whom

"the duality of the physical and the mental is integrated at the level of self-conscious mind or spirit." [69]

If it defies our best efforts to understand fully the body-mind or brain-mind relationship, even to the extent that some waver between seeing them (it) as dualistic or monistic, how much more difficult it is to understand the whole complexity of the total man. I do not profess to understand this. My point of departure is simply in what I believe to be the Biblical perspective, which requires that we see man in a polar situation, as both aspective and unitary or holistic—aspective but not dualistic or partitive, holistic but not monistic. Whatever is there in man is there holistically, subject to analysis but not to dissection or extraction.

Chapter 3

INDIVIDUAL
YET CORPORATE

Man finds his true existence in the polarity of solitude and solidarity,[1] individuality and community. As an individual he has an identity never to be confused with another. As a person he is necessarily in a bundle with God and his fellowmen. Individuality is that which distinguishes a man from God and from other men and gives him identity and uniqueness. It cries out against every kind of stereotyping, whether racial, class, caste, sexual, age group, or some other kind. Personhood is that which vitally relates him to God and other persons. Man is not an island, for no man lives or dies unto himself (Rom. 14:7). Neither is man a part of a machine or a spark ultimately to be reabsorbed into a cosmic flame (Stoicism). If man is to be truly man, he cannot escape the tension of this polarity. That he finds his true being in this polarity is the perspective of Scripture throughout.

As is true of man in his other polar situations, he rebels against the one or the other here, either against his dependence upon others or his own solitude. The Stoic ideal was ultimate absorption of the human soul, a spark, back into the cosmic flame, with total loss of individual identity. This goal of mystical absorption is the ideal of various Oriental cults. Nirvana is the next thing to complete absorption; it is a passive state in which the soul is just that but no more. At the other extreme is the goal of independence. This is the Western mania with its egotistical nonsense about the "self-made" man, "beholden to no one," the man who is "master of his own fate."

There are ample followers of each cult, that of rugged individualism trying to be an island and that of mystical absorption. Either may be philosophical-religious or practical-secular. All totalitarianism, e.g., sacrifices the individual to the state; and the naïve capitalist thinks that he can build his own little isolationist world and live within it, gathering about himself wealth and "security" in the midst of poverty. Scripture rejects both illusions—that one can live alone or that he must lose his identity. Scripture keeps us in the tension of individuality without which we are lost and community without which we are equally lost.

INDIVIDUAL IDENTITY

We are created, called, redeemed, and ultimately resurrected as individuals. This is the Biblical perspective. Even in a population explosion, we are born individually. In the human race there are no duplicates, no carbon copies. Each is an original. We did not come off an assembly line, nor were we run off on a printing press or mimeograph machine. Not even "identical twins" are identical. Each of us has his own fingerprints and even his own voiceprint. Each voice makes its own distinctive graph when electronically recorded and can be thus identified from among any number of other voices. We may try to surrender our identity through imitation of others, but birth did not design us as "copy cats." Others may try to reduce us to some form of stereotype, but we were not intended for such loss of identity.

We sometimes say of an unusual person, "When they made him they broke the mold." That may be said of *each* human being. No two are made in the same mold. One may surrender his uniqueness in his desire to conform to those about him, or other people may try to deny or to destroy individuality in another. Even within community as primary as family or church, individuality is not to be sacrificed. It is rather to be enhanced.

In sin and salvation alike, individuality is there, however far society or culture may mold us or however great may be the weight of history and humanity upon us. Sometimes the forces of history and humanity almost crush us, but man is never totally victimized by outside forces. His sin is not in what others do to him but in what he *lets* them do to him. Forces outside us can do much to us without our permission, but there is that which cannot be done to us apart from our consent or response. You may be able to strike me without my consent or cooperation, but you cannot make me angry or make me hate without some measure of my consent. I am not responsible for what you do to me; I am responsible for what I *let* you do to me. However much another may contribute to my sinning, in the final analysis it is I who sin. Sometimes the forces from without may be so overpowering that the heaviest guilt is upon those who crush me, but no one of us can "pass the buck" completely to history or humanity. It is a part of being human that even in sin I have my measure of identity, freedom, and sovereignty.

In salvation as in sin, individuality is inescapably present. Salvation in the Biblical sense, or in any meaningful sense, is utterly impossible apart from individual freedom. One cannot begin to be saved as a human being if his identity is ignored, denied, or overrun. This is the fallacy of "predestination." The doctrine that God can arbitrarily call some to salvation and leave others to damnation is untrue to Scripture, but it also is inherently false. "Salvation" by determination would not be salvation at all. It would be damnation raised to the nth degree. God calls each one individually, each one by name. But he calls us as individual persons. He does not move us like pawns on a chessboard or manipulate us like machines. Never does God override our individuality, including freedom of consent, even in salvation.

Individuality is respected in the initiation of salvation, and it is cultivated throughout salvation. God is the God of Abraham, of Isaac, of Jacob, not just of the nation Israel. God spoke to Abraham by name. He called the lad Samuel by name. He called Andrew and Peter, James and John individually; and he calls us individually. Individuality is heightened in salvation, not

destroyed, diminished, or obscured. Abraham, Isaac, and Jacob
grew in their individuality in the company of God and God's
people. Peter's rugged individuality grew stronger in discipleship. Individuation and maturation belong properly to growth in
salvation.

Jesus' Respect for Individuality. One can get lost in a
crowd, and some people never see the individual within the
crowd. Jesus not only wept over the crowds of people (cf. Matt.
9:35–38), but he could also single out the individual, no matter
how great the crowd around him (cf. John 5:1–9). There is an
old proverb which charges that some people "cannot see the
woods for the trees," i.e., they cannot see the wholeness of something because of the parts. Is it not equally true that sometimes
we do not see the trees for the woods? One may so narrow his
vision to a single tree that he fails to see the forest. He also may
be so overpowered by the forest that he does not see single trees
in their individuality. Jesus was able to see both "the woods"
and "the trees," the vast throngs of people about him and also
the individual persons who made up those crowds.

When Jesus saw "the crowds" he was moved with compassion
(Matt. 9:36). He saw them as "harassed and helpless," as sheep
without the loving care of a shepherd. It is a judgment upon the
religious establishment of the day that the crowds lacked such
care, for religion was outwardly robust. The Temple was crowded
with pilgrims from all over the Greco-Roman world, and there
were thousands of priests who in two-week rotations kept up the
cultic practices at the Temple. There were in addition many
rabbis among the Pharisees, laymen who made the study of the
Law their first interest. With the leaders of the Qumran group,
probably Essenes, and other sectarian groups, there were thus
thousands of people concerned intensely with religion. The people,
however, were neglected at the level of their daily needs. Many
failed to see the crowds as they focused on the forms of religion.
Jesus did not fail to see them and to have compassion for them.

Jesus saw the crowds and had compassion on them not only at
the level of their "moral and spiritual" needs, but in relation to
their sicknesses and hunger. He responded to the maimed, the

blind, the deaf (Matt. 15:30 f.), and the hungry (Matt. 15:32). He agonized over the crowds and over the difficulty of ministering to them. His impulse was to give them all they asked, yet he repeatedly found it necessary to withdraw from them as they tried to force him into Messianic patterns which he was compelled to reject (cf. John 6:15).

But Jesus saw "the trees" as well as "the woods." He could see the individual person, however insignificant he seemed to be or however big the crowd. He gladly received the little children even though his disciples impatiently tried to send them away (Matt. 19:13–15). At the pool of Bethzatha in Jerusalem, where there was a multitude of sick people, he could single out an individual, as in the case of a man who had been lame for thirty-eight years (John 5:2–9). In Jericho he could bring into direct, personal focus the despised tax collector Zacchaeus, even in the midst of a massive crowd (Luke 19:1–10). Jesus startled the crowd and amazed Peter when he responded to the touch of a poor woman who for twelve years had suffered a hemorrhage (Luke 8:42b–48). He singled her out and for a moment at least gave her his full attention, even as the multitudes surrounded him and pressed upon him. Jesus could watch the multitude putting money in the Temple treasury, and see not only many rich putting in large sums but a poor widow with "two copper coins" (Mark 12:41–44). He came to create a new people of God, but he went about it by addressing individual persons: James and John, Andrew and Peter, Matthew the taxgatherer, and many others.

The regard Jesus had for individual dignity and freedom comes out in several Gospel stories. One of the more instructive is that of a visit in the home of Mary and Martha (Luke 10:38–42). Martha was hostess to Jesus and becoming "distracted with much serving." While Mary sat listening to Jesus, she complained to Jesus that he had not told her sister to assist her with the serving. Jesus defended Mary in her choice of "the good portion." The story's main point may be that there is "food" more important even than that for the body (cf. John 4:32), but the fact remains that Jesus did defend Mary's right to her own individuality. He refused to support Martha in her attempt to force Mary into a

"Martha" role. It was proper for Martha to be Martha, but it was wrong for her to try to compel Mary to become "Martha" or "Martha the second." Mary not only had chosen "the better part," but it was Mary's right to choose her part, not to be forced into Martha's choice.

Suppose the "shoe" had been on the other foot? Suppose Mary had made a slighting remark about her sister Martha in her preoccupation with the meal? She could have said to Jesus: "Just look at my old sister! Here I am improving my mind and giving attention to 'spiritual' things, but my old mundane sister is content just to serve a meal." Had Mary so spoken, would not Jesus have shielded Martha against Mary? He probably would have said: "Mary, you let Martha alone. You have chosen your part. Let her choose hers. Besides, I am hungry and when she gets it on the table I am going to eat!" The point is that Martha and Mary, sisters with very close ties (cf. John 11:1–44), were distinct individuals and Jesus respected the identity and dignity of each.

Peter and John were two of Jesus' closest disciples, and they too were respected by Jesus in their own individuality. Jesus called them individually and by name, and their individuality was protected to the end. Jesus sought out Peter after Peter's shameful denial of his master, confronting him with the discrepancy between proud boasts and poor performance, but also recommissioning him to his ministry (John 21:15–19). When Peter was warned about the prospect of martyrdom as the price of discipleship, Peter turned to John and asked what his lot would be (John 21:20 f.). Jesus then told Peter in no uncertain terms that John's lot was not Peter's business (John 21:22). Each was called to fulfill his own ministry, even if for one it meant martyrdom and for the other living on until the parousia. This was not a matter of favoritism. It was a matter of individuality—to each his life to live, his ministry to fulfill.

Jesus had compassion for the crowds but also brought the individual into sharpest focus. Jesus reminded his disciples that not a sparrow falls to the ground without God's notice and that even the hairs of one's head are numbered (Matt. 10:29–31). He assured them that they were of infinitely more worth than sparrows. The importance of even one is clearly implied in the parable of the lost sheep, where ninety-nine sheep safely in the fold do not lessen the shepherd's concern for the one that is missing (Matt. 18:12; Luke 15:4, 7). God cares for "the last and the least." Each is of infinite worth.

It is sometimes held that it was at the point of accountability that the individual first emerged in Hebrew concern, the earlier stress being upon the solidarity of the family, tribe, or nation. This probably cannot be demonstrated, for alongside the emphasis upon solidarity was also the recognition of the individual. God was known as the God of Abraham, God of Isaac, and God of Jacob, not just God of Israel (cf. Gen. 32:9; Ex. 3:15; 6:2 f., 8, and *passim*). But probably it was at the point of accountability that the individual was brought into sharper focus. A deepening sense of morality developed in Israel along with a new emphasis upon the individual person, and this is closely bound up with prophetic reformation in Israel, from Elijah through Amos, Hosea, Isaiah, Micah, Jeremiah, and Ezekiel.[2] One such expression may be seen in Deut. 24:16: "The fathers shall not be put to death for the children, nor shall the children be put to death for the fathers; every man shall be put to death for his own sin."

James warns that the Lord of Sabaoth sees those who hold back the wages of the laborers, and he hears the cries of the harvesters who have gone unpaid (James 5:4). Jesus made our treatment of "the least" of his "brethren" the ultimate test in the final judgment (Matt. 25:40, 45). How we treat one another in the commonplaces of life, as where there is hunger or sickness, matters eternally. Christ sees these people and we dare not fail to see them also. There is no more tender passage in Scripture than the picture in Revelation of God's wiping away "every tear" from the eyes of his people who on earth have suffered for him (Rev. 7:17; 21:4). All matter to God, and each matters to God.

Individuality Beyond Death. People often ask, "Will we know one another in heaven?" The longing to know and to be known begins at the outset of this life, and it is coveted for the life beyond death. Except where anonymity is thought essential to security, people generally want to be known, by name and in terms of their individuality. There are people who have been so oppressed or threatened by society that they seek refuge in anonymity. This is seen especially among minority groups. Many Europeans, for example, have changed their names upon coming to America, this to escape the abuses and dangers their racial or national group had known in the older country. In a pattern born out of oppression, many black people through past generations and even into the present protect themselves and their neighbors by not disclosing their identity or that of their neighbors to unidentified strangers. Any stranger, especially white, could represent a threat. With the contemporary assault on privacy, massive snooping and secret records by governmental agencies and credit houses, the whole public may find it necessary to seek refuge in anonymity (cf. the appeal of the condominium). There is nothing new about seeking security through anonymity. This is an ancient practice, for if one's name were known he could suffer direct oppression or another might evoke some divine or demonic curse upon him. The New Testament Apocalypse was written in a time of persecution, and this illuminates the promise to the faithful at Pergamum: "I will give him a white stone, with a new name written on the stone which no one knows except him who receives it" (Rev. 2:17).

But this premuim on anonymity is by no means the whole story. In wider Biblical perspective, there is great concern to know and be known. The "knowledge of God" with "steadfast love" is desired rather than "sacrifice" and "burnt offerings" (Hos. 6:6). Isaiah anticipated the coming of "a shoot from the stump of Jesse" with the result that "the earth shall be full of the knowledge of the Lord" (Isa. 11:9). Man's fatal mistake is his choice not to have God in his knowledge (cf. Rom. 1:28; I Cor. 15:34). Paul's prayer for the Colossians was that they be "increasing in the knowledge of God" (Col. 1:10). Grace and peace are multiplied "in the knowledge of God and of Jesus our Lord" (II Peter 1:2). Except where threatened, people universally want to be known and known by name.

There is no explicit Biblical discussion of the recognizability of the dead, but the implications are solidly in that direction. In the transfiguration scene, Moses and Elijah are recognized as such (Mark 9:4 f.). Likewise, in the story of the rich man and Lazarus, each person appears beyond death in recognizable form. Lazarus and Abraham are called by name, and the rich man and Lazarus address one another across the gulf that separates them (Luke 16:19–31). Even if this be taken as a parable, it yet assumes that persons are recognized by name beyond death. Stephen as he died cried out that he saw "the Son of man standing at the right hand of God" (Acts 7:56). If we are not known beyond death, then we are not *we*. One's identity, that which distinguishes him from all others, belongs to his essence. In creation or birth, in salvation, and in eternity one has his identity or he has nothing.

PERSONS IN COMMUNITY

Cyprian, bishop of Carthage (d. 258), is often quoted for his statement *"Extra ecclesiam nulla salus"* ("Outside the church there is no salvation"). Properly understood, this claim is profoundly true, whatever may have been Cyprian's intention. If by "church" is meant not an ecclesiastical organization or institution but the people or family of God, the statement is sound and significant. It belongs to the essence of lostness to be alone, cut off from meaningful relationship with God, cut off from other people, from things, and even from self. It belongs to the essence of salvation to belong and to enjoy meaningful relationship with God, with other people, with things, and with oneself. In this sense, there is no salvation outside "the church," the people of God. To say that one cannot "be saved" in isolation is to say that one cannot be a real person, an authentic human being, alone.

Just as individuality has to do with one's distinction from all others, so one's personhood has to do with his relatedness. Much that belongs essentially to personhood implies relationship: love, trust, acceptance, commitment, confession, forgiveness, etc. Paul was pleading for respect for individual differences when he said,

"None of us lives to himself, and none of us dies to himself" (Rom. 14:7), but in so doing he accentuated our dependence upon others and our relatedness to them. We live unto the Lord and we die unto the Lord, for we belong unto the Lord (Rom. 14:8). We are to make room for individual conscience (Rom. 14:5), accepting one another even though we may differ in beliefs and practices (Rom. 14:2). Individual identity, integrity, and freedom are to be granted to one another, and this is bound up with the fact that together we belong to the same Lord and answer to him.

Berdyaev was profoundly right in declaring, "Where there is no God there is no man." [3] By this he meant that one cannot be an authentic person apart from God. Man is not God, and it is idolatry to see oneself as God. On the other hand, man cannot become himself except in meaningful relationship with God. Man is more than *homo sapiens,* having rationality. He is more than *homo faber,* man as maker or doer. He is also *homo orans,* man as worshiper. Man is incomplete without God. Augustine was correct in saying that man was made for God and that he is restless until he rests in God (cf. Acts 17:26–28 for a similar view). This need not imply that man takes the initiative in seeking God, but it does mean that in man as man there is that which cannot find fulfillment apart from God. Physically, man is a very small creature, but in his true dimensions he reaches out far beyond his physical world and even that of all space and time. He cannot be contained within these limits. His true being calls for eternity and infinity—this without the sacrifice of his individual, bodily existence (see below on "body").

As person, man cannot find fulfillment apart from other human beings. This is why "the God of Abraham, Isaac, and Jacob" is also the creator of "Israel." This is why he who called Peter, James, and John also created the church. One may be lost alone but not saved in aloneness. One may be a fraction of a self or a "torso" alone, but he cannot be a person alone. No one has brought this out better than John Baillie, through his own thought and by bringing together the thinking of others on this subject. [4] He, with agreement, finds that "the whole of Professor Heidegger's philosophy rests on the realization that *'alles Dasein ist Mitsein'*—*'all existence is coexistence.'* "[5] Martin Buber put it thus: *"Ich werde am Du; alles wirkliche Leben ist Begegnung"* ("I come into being over against the Thou; all real life is of the nature of encounter").[6] Only in the presence of God and other people does one emerge as a true person. Gogarten wrote in similar fashion, *"Ich bin durch dich"* ("I am through you").[7] All these men were recognizing our dependence upon others for our true being. The potential becomes real only as we interact with or enter into community with other persons.

Corporate Personality in the Old Testament. In the ancient world to which the Hebrew people belonged, there was an idea of "corporate personality."[8] In much primitive legislation and religion men were dealt with not in terms of their individuality but as members of a family, clan, or tribe. The sin of one was seen to pervade his whole group, and revenge was sought from the whole group rather than the single offender. This view of "corporate personality" may be traced in the Old Testament along with the emergence of a new emphasis upon the individual.

As we have seen, accountability or moral responsibility is the primary focal point for the movement from the idea of "corporate personality" to individualism. For primitive man collective responsibility was the controlling idea, and the consciousness of individuality, the "I," remained weak and underdeveloped.[9] In Israel, it was chiefly through the prophets that the individual was distinguished from the group, especially at the point of accountability. Not only was the individual not to bear the blame for the tribe but especially was he not to escape accountability by "passing the buck" to his forebears. With a growing emphasis upon individual responsibility was a fuller personal consciousness awakened.

The idea of corporate solidarity is reflected in the customs of blood revenge, where a whole family or clan was held responsible for the deed of one of their members (cf. I Sam. 15:3; II Sam. 14:7; 21:1–14). This may be seen also in the practice of Levirate marriage (Deut. 25:5), where a man is regarded as identical with his dead brother.[10] With this is the idea of the visitation of the sins of the fathers upon their children to the third or fourth generation (Ex. 20:5; cf. II Kings 9:26). Most instructive is the story of Achan (Josh. 7:24–26), whose sin of theft and breaking of a taboo affected all of Israel.

The Hebrew word *adam* now conjures up for us the image of a single individual, but in its Old Testament usage *adam* means primarily mankind and only in a secondary sense does it denote an individual man.[11] This is apparent in Gen. 5:2.

> This is the book of the generations of Adam. When God created man, he made him in the likeness of God. Male and female he created them, and he blessed them and named them Man when they were created. (Gen. 5:1, 2.)

The Hebrew *adam* is clearly used for "man" or "mankind" in this passage. In the next verse (Gen. 5:3), *adam* refers to an individual person. Probably Paul's "in Adam" refers to one's being a part of the human race in its natural condition, just as "in Christ" denotes one's participation in the church as the body of Christ (cf. I Cor. 15:22).

This passage (I Cor. 15:22) has served as a basic proof text for the view that all humanity inherited Adam's sin, either because when the "head of the race" sinned all sinned (the "federal" theory of original sin) or because we were in the loins of Adam (Augustine's theory). Augustine's theory is based more on Rom. 5:12, where the Greek *eph hō* is mistranslated into Latin as *in quo,* "in whom," instead of "inasmuch as" or "because." In Rom. 5:12, Paul gives the equation: one man sinned and he died . . . death spread to all because *all* sinned. Augustine twisted this equation: one man sinned and he died . . . death spread to all because *one* sinned! Fortunately we still have Paul's own way of stating it.

Returning to I Cor. 15:22, one may derive from it the popular idea of "original sin" only by doing violence to Paul. The two parts of the verse may not be divorced. Between them is a comparison, "just as" (*hōsper*) . . . "thus also" (*houtōs kai*). We die "in Adam" the way we live "in Christ." Does Paul imply universal salvation when he writes, "Thus also in Christ all shall be saved"? His strenuous mission and agony over his people do not support this interpretation (cf. Rom. 9:1–5, 31 f.; 10:1–3, 21). Paul does not mean that all men are automatically lost because Adam sinned any more than that all are automatically saved because Jesus came, lived, died, and arose. He means that to be "in Adam" is to die just as to be "in Christ" is to live. We share the fate or destiny of the one to whom we yield, Adam or Christ. To be "in Christ" is to be joined to Jesus Christ but thus also to his people, the church as the body of Christ (I Cor. 12:12 f.). Likewise, to be "in Adam" is to be joined to humanity outside Christ. One is in solidarity with Christ or Adam, with humanity reconciled to God or humanity estranged from God.

Although the Hebrew people for a time seemingly shared with the larger primitive world its view of "corporate personality," this view was at a very early time modified by concern also with the individual person. Eichrodt views Ex., chs. 20 to 23, as the "Book of the Covenant" and sees it as going back at least to the time of the entry of the Israelites into the Promised Land, with codification of still earlier customs, and as relating the protection afforded by the Law to the community as a whole with the claim made on the Law by the individual.[12] Collective retribution as a principle of punishment no longer played a part in this covenant code, although legal retribution still utilized the idea of solidarity of guilt in the family (cf. II Sam., ch. 21). In the code the individual is singled out for responsibility, and the commands are directed to the individual Israelite: "You shall not . . ." (Ex. 20:13–17).[13]

With the balancing of individuality with corporateness is also an emphasis upon knowledge and intention in questions of individual accountability. Guilt came to be seen not as some "objective fate" which may engulf the whole group but as a matter of personal and conscious responsibility. Instead of "guilt by association," guilt was seen as implying a moral subject, responsible for his action. Guilt implied the individual's knowledge and intention behind his action. With this deeper understanding of sin and guilt as growing out of the heart or mind of the individual came the plea for a law "written on the heart" and little confidence in "justice imposed by law." Even Leviticus, with its priestly concern for cultic functions, knows the importance of individual decision.[14] Hebrew "corporateness," then, at no time proved to be a mere "collectivism," for the Law in its various expressions always was concerned to awaken a sense of personal responsibility in each individual.[15]

A balanced view between corporateness and individuality is to be seen then in the Old Testament, with the movement not from the individual to the group but the reverse. It probably is too much to say that the Hebrew people ever completely neglected the individual in favor of a "collective," at least not as traceable in the Old Testament. But there was a strong emphasis upon the group. Beginning with Abraham, at least, is the strong emphasis upon the creation of the people of God. When God called Abraham to go out from his "country," his "kindred," and his "father's house," it was with the promise that God would make him "a great nation" (Gen. 12:1–2). This promise was renewed when Abraham and Lot separated, the Lord promising "that Abraham shall become a great and mighty nation" (Gen. 18:18).

Although the focus is upon the promised "nation," there are in fact two foci: Abraham and the nation. God did not call the nation Israel. He called Abraham. Later he called Isaac and Jacob, and still later he called Moses and Samuel. God called individuals and kept calling individuals. He called them to become Israel. This foreshadows the New Testament pattern. God did not call the church; he creates it. He called Andrew and Peter, James and John, Stephen and Saul, and countless other individuals to become the church. Thus individuality and corporateness belong together in proper balance. This conception emerges in the Old Testament and continues throughout the New.

THE PEOPLE OF GOD

There is no one dominant term for the Biblical view of man in his relatedness. Possibly "the people of God" serves as well as any to designate the relationship which under God we may have with one another (cf. Judg. 20:2; II Sam. 14:13; Ps. 47:9; Heb. 4:9; 11:25; I Peter 2:10). In the New Testament this relationship of persons is known as the church, the body of Christ, followers of the Way, the flock, the family of God, etc. Various terms and analogies serve to bring out the many-sided nature of this mutuality of life shared by God and his people. In this corporateness of the people of God individuality is not lost. It is heightened. Paul does not become Apollos and Apollos does not become Paul. Neither becomes Jesus and Jesus does not become either. The identity, integrity, dignity, and freedom of each is respected. But with this each moves toward fulfillment in a relationship which is so close that what happens to one happens to each and all. To sin against one is to sin against all. To serve one is to serve all.

On This Rock. Matt. 16:18 has long been a controversial text, a point of sharp debate. This was especially so in the older days when Roman Catholics and Protestants pressed their rival claims against one another. There doubtless is more light in the passage for all of us when we put aside partisan claims and try to give ourselves in new openness to what the text would say to us. Whatever may be the precise reference in "this rock," the passage does focus attention on both individuality and community. It sees Jesus as building his church in a way that preserves the identity of both Jesus and Peter—and you and me.

To the question, "Who do men say that the Son of man is?" various answers were given: John the Baptist, Elijah, Jeremiah, or one of the prophets. Jesus rejected all of these answers. He was not John the Baptist. John was John. No one else was John and John was no one else. Elijah was Elijah, only he and none else. None else was he. Jeremiah was Jeremiah. Only he and none other. "One of the prophets?" Mr. Anonymous! No, Jesus was not Mr. Anonymous, not even "one of the prophets." He was Jesus Christ. He was none other and none other was he. This was most important. Peter and all must look at Jesus and see him—see him in his own identity, not confused with any other.

Jesus then said, "And I tell you, you are Peter." Jesus saw

Peter for who he was and for what he was. He did not look at
Peter and see John. He did not ask Peter to become John. Peter
had his own identity, his own individuality, his own strength, and
his own weakness. Jesus accepted Peter as Peter, not as someone else. Here is where it begins: "You are the Christ, the Son
of the living God" (Matt. 16:16), and "You are Peter" (Matt.
16:18). On this rock Jesus Christ can build the church. The
church is where Christ, you, and I meet, each open to the other,
each accepting the other in terms of who he is. In this very act
of mutual acceptance and commitment the church comes into being. It is the church, a corporate relationship, a family, the people
of God. It is not a mere collection of individuals. It is a mystery
and miracle of the solidarity of Christ and his people in a relationship which preserves, frees, and heightens the individuality
of each.

The English word "church" probably comes from the Greek
kyriakos, "belonging to the Lord." If so, it sees us as made one
people under the Lordship of Christ. It sees us as joined together as we come one by one to acknowledge the same claim
upon ourselves—the claim of Jesus Christ as ultimate and absolute. We do not live up to but we do live under such a claim.
It is this which unites us and binds us to one another as it binds
us to him.

The New Testament word for "church" is *ekklēsia,* a word
which in its etymology means "called out." Probably in its
Biblical usage it stresses not only the fact of our being "elected"
or "called out" but also the fact that we belong to the Lord.
Jesus spoke of "my church" (Matt. 16:18). We are his people.
Thus the English word "church" is derived from some word
other than *ekklēsia,* but happily it captures much of the intention
of the Biblical *ekklēsia.*

The church is not the kingdom (local or universal), nor is
the kingdom the church. They are related but not identical. The
kingdom is the sovereign rule of God. It means that God is
king. Jesus Christ is God's Christ, God's anointed. In Jesus
Christ the kingdom of God comes to us with the summons to
repent, to turn, to trust, to obey, to come under his sovereign

claim. The kingdom is—with or without our permission. The kingdom *comes*. The church must *become*. The church is a community of persons brought together under one sovereign claim of Jesus Christ. Apart from this sovereignty we are separated, estranged, alone. Under this claim we are brought together—Jew and Gentile, bond and free, male and female, black and white. Jesus Christ is the hope God holds out for our being brought together into one new humanity (cf. Eph. 3:1–13; 4:1–16).

But the church is not only a unity; it is the preservation of individuality. The kingdom of God is the sovereignty under which we are brought together, but in that solidarity we find our individual identity, integrity, and freedom. Jesus declared that men would come from East and West and sit with Abraham, Isaac, and Jacob. The church is the people of God, drawn together out of widely different backgrounds and made into one family; but although their hostilities, fears, jealousies, prejudices, and the like are overcome, they retain their own individualities.

The Flock. Flocks and herds played an important role in the life of the Jews and their ancestors, and pastoral images and themes abound in their worship and thought (cf. Psalm 23). Jesus drew upon this heritage in speaking of his people as his flock (cf. Luke 12:32). It was his concern that we be "one flock" under the care of "one shepherd" (John 10:16). The term for some time continued to be applied to the church (cf. Acts 20:28 f.; I Cor. 9:7; I Peter 5:2 f.).

Along with the oneness of the flock was the preservation of the individual. A good shepherd "calls his own sheep by name" (John 10:3). Each individual sheep is precious. A shepherd with a hundred sheep is not content to find only ninety-nine safe in the fold (Luke 15:4–7). He doesn't say, "Well, you win some and lose some." If one is missing, he searches for it until he finds it, and finding it gives him greater joy than he can contain alone, so he has to call in the neighbors to help him enjoy his joy. The value of one is not forgotten in concern for the oneness of the flock. Corporateness and individuality belong together.

The Body of Christ. Paul's great analogy for the church was "the body of Christ." He never speaks of "a body of Christians" but rather of the church as Christ's own body. The oneness of this body is such to Paul that what happens to any Christian happens to Christ. To divide the church is to divide Christ (I Cor. 1:13). To sin against a weaker brother is to sin against Christ (I Cor. 8:12). Paul probably learned this lesson on the Damascus road, for the Christ who appeared to him there did so in relationship with his church.[16] Paul (Saul) had been persecuting the church, but Jesus asked, "Saul, Saul, why do you persecute me?" (Acts 9:4). In persecuting Christians, Saul persecuted Christ.

In developing this analogy, Paul was concerned to keep in balance the individuality of each Christian and the corporate unity of the whole church. In I Cor., ch. 12, Paul presses these points with utmost care. He holds in balance the unity of the body and the plurality and variety of its members. Paul declares that the body is one yet has many members (I Cor. 12:12). Just as strongly, he insists that the body does not consist of one member (I Cor. 12:14). His point is that the church must be Christ's own body, that it must be a relationship of unbroken unity, and that the identity, dignity, and freedom of each member must be preserved. The eye is the only member of the body that can see, so its individuality is of ultimate worth. At the same time, the eye can find fulfillment in the power to see only as it finds its place within the body. Again, in Romans, Paul gives equal stress to corporate unity and individual identity:

> For as in one body we have many members, and all the members do not have the same function, so we, though many, are one body in Christ, and individually members one of another. (Rom. 12:4 f.)

He continues the twin emphasis in pointing to various "gifts" (prophecy, service, teaching, exhortation, etc.) which are to be exercised freely within the oneness of the church.

Wayne Oates finds an instructive example of the recognition of "the wholeness of personality, opposed to its division and adulteration," in the logion about the eye as the lamp of the body (Matt. 6:22–23).[17] If the eye is "light," the *whole body* is filled with light; if it is dark, the *whole body* is in darkness. He concludes, "The part has no meaning apart from the whole organism, and the whole organism is dependent on the part." [18]

Koinōnia of the Spirit. The *koinōnia* of the Spirit is a fellowship that preserves the polarity of individuality in solidarity. Barth states it cogently:

> It is . . . not a communion in which the "otherness" of each particular individual is blurred or limited or dissolved, but that *oneness* which both requires the "otherness" of each individual and makes sense of it. Fellowship is the *One* which lies beyond every "other" . . . not a cell in a larger organism, but simply the *Holy One*—sanctus.[19]

Paul, John, and Acts make much of *koinōnia* in the early church. *Koinōnia* designates what two or more have in common. To be called by God into Christian discipleship is to be "called into the fellowship of his Son, Jesus Christ our Lord" (I Cor. 1:9). "Fellowship" translates *koinōnia* and means more than normally is connoted by the English word "fellowship." Paul's idea is that of a common life, of our participating together in the very life of Jesus Christ. He sees "the cup" and "the loaf" as meaningful only as they reflect our joint participation in the life and body of Christ (I Cor. 10:16–17).

John sees this *koinōnia* with God and with his people as the end goal of all preaching (I John 1:1–3). The goal of redemption and of preaching is that we have *koinōnia* with one another by entering together in the life eternal which was with the Father and which penetrated history and flesh in the person of Jesus Christ. God's kind of existence penetrated history and bodily existence in Jesus so tangibly that it could be seen, heard, and touched with our hands. God's work of redemption is to bring us out of our aloneness into this shared life. To be saved, then, is to be joined together under the Lordship of Christ (I Cor. 1:9) in God's kind of existence, that which took shape in the bodily, historical existence of Jesus Christ (I John 1:1–3).

The *koinōnia* of the Holy Spirit (II Cor. 13:14) means more than cooperation, agreement, or the world's kind of "fellowship." Cooperation is in itself neither good nor bad. Sometimes it is better not to cooperate than to cooperate, as when the cause is evil. Cooperation is only as good as are the motives behind it and the goals before it. Gangsters cooperate in robbing a bank, and the parts of a motor cooperate (work together) without knowing what they are doing. *Koinōnia* is more than cooperation. It is also more than agreement. Men may agree in error and evil as well as in truth and right. In the book of Acts it is said that Christians were of "one accord" (*homothumadon*) in prayer (Acts 1:14), in awaiting the day of Pentecost (Acts 2:1), in attending the Temple together (Acts 2:46), in praying for the release of Peter and John (Acts 4:24), in banding together in Solomon's porch in a time of persecution (Acts 5:12), and in their agreement at the apostolic council during a time of controversy (Acts 15:25). The identical word is used to describe such evil actions as the murderous assault upon Stephen (Acts 7:57), the hypocrisy in flattering Herod Agrippa (Acts 12:20), the united attack upon Paul (Acts 18:12), and the rush of a mad mob into a theater in Ephesus (Acts 19:29).[20] The *koinōnia* of the Holy Spirit is not just the world's kind of joining together in work or play. It is being joined together in the kind of existence which comes from God and which makes us one people under one ultimate and absolute claim, that of the kingdom of God as it confronts us in Jesus Christ. It is in this *koinōnia* that "our joy may be complete" (I John 1:4), for it is in this *koinōnia* that we as persons become complete.

The *koinōnia* of the Spirit means corporateness so real that what happens to one happens to all. This comes to poignant expression in Philemon. Paul pleads for the release of a runaway slave, now a Christian brother. He says to the slave's master, "So if you consider me your partner, receive him as you would receive me" (Philemon, v. 17). "Partner" translates *koinōnon*. Strictly rendered, Paul's plea is "receive him as me." Onesimus is Paul, in a real sense. What happens to Onesimus happens to Paul. To receive Onesimus is to receive Paul; to reject Onesimus is to reject Paul. Of course the identity of each—Paul, Onesimus, and the owner—is preserved. Each comes into sharp focus as an individual. But Paul also stresses their solidarity. As individuals they are distinguishable each from the other. As persons they are so related that what affects one affects all.

The idea of *koinōnia* is unusually prominent in Philippians. This great church, for all its compassion and unselfish service, was threatened by disunity. Euodia and Syntyche had fallen out (Phil. 4:2), and there was murmuring and disputing in the church (Phil. 2:14). A major purpose of the letter is to plead for unity in the church. Paul's hope for such unity is based on a number of considerations, prominent among which was the "*koinōnia* in the Spirit" (Phil. 2:1). Paul was not asking for stereotype or uniformity. He was calling for unity in love and purpose. With full allowance made for individual difference, Paul says Christian discipleship necessarily implies corporate unity. It is not so much that we as Christians ought to become one people. If Christian, we *are* one people—the *koinōnia* created by the Spirit of God under the Lordship of Christ. This will find outward expression in the sharing of material substance as it is needed (Acts 2:42; 4:32; II Cor. 8:4; Rom. 15:26 f.; Phil. 1:5; 4:15). It means separation from the world (I John 1:6 ff.). It means unity with one another (Phil. 2:1 ff.). It means acceptance of one another (Philemon, vs. 6, 17). It means suffering together (Phil. 3:10; 4:14; I Peter 4:13). It means joy together (I John 1:4).

This is our existence as Christians, in the polarity of solitude and solidarity, individuality and community. In this is our true selfhood brought to fulfillment. In thus "losing" ourselves to Christ and his people we find ourselves. As in marriage "the two become one flesh" (the two paradoxically become "one" yet remain "two"), so in Christ we are "one body" yet retain or find our true individual identity in that union.

Chapter 4

MADE
TO BECOME

"Already but not yet" is a phrase often applied to a certain understanding of the kingdom of God, inaugurated in the ministry of Jesus but awaiting its consummation at his parousia.[1] The phrase could be applied to a person under redemption. He is but he also must become. A Christian is a person in the making. Christianity was first known as "the Way" (Acts 9:2; 22:4; 24:14, 22). It is a pilgrimage (Heb., chs. 12; 13). One may be seen as saved (Luke 19:9), as being saved (I Cor. 1:18), and as awaiting his salvation (Rom. 13:11).

Heschel puts it in right perspective when he describes the "nonfinality" of man, rarely found in a "definitive edition," never found in final and permanent form, "caught in the polarity of being both tentative, undecided, unsettled" and at the same time "final, fixed, and determined."[2] Man is found in a state of flux, a *status nascendi*. He is a person in the making, a pilgrim on the way. Being human is a goal as well as an achievement, an opportunity as well as a fact.[3] Oates holds that "man from his conception to his death, experiences himself both as a *being self* and as a *becoming self,* as an actual and as a potential person."[4] As Ernst Käsemann reads the apostle Paul, Paul sees man—by whatever else determined—as "a challengeable and continually challenged being." And this is "a constitutive part of his existence," for "man is always faced with a call," experiencing "the divine address," which means that "he stands beneath the sign of exodus and his horizon is hope" (cf. Gen., ch. 12; Heb., ch. 12).[5]

Throughout the Old and New Testaments man is continually called to decision.[6] He is addressed as one who has certain freedom of choice and who must bear the responsibility of making choices which affect his being and existence. This concentration upon decision implies that man is "made to become," that the kind of person he becomes depends in part upon what he does with his options. God does not thrust upon man a certain character or kind of existence, although he makes possible the options from which man is to choose. Genetics and environment have much to do with man's possibilities, but they alone do not determine the man. Man may resist all that would shape him or he may allow himself to be shaped by these forces and factors. Over genetics he may have little or no control; as for environment, he may rebel against it or succumb to it.

God's Creative Work

Man is made to become, but he cannot become through himself alone. He cannot so transcend himself as to be able to lift himself by his own bootstraps (Rom. 7:7–25). He can become only in response to God who addresses him, calls to him from without (Rom., ch. 8). When man becomes an authentic human being, it is the result of God's own creative work, calling man to an existence which moves in the direction of an essence which is from God (I Cor. 15:10; Gal. 2:20; Eph. 2:10).

There is a sense in which man in salvation is created *ex nihilo,* "out of nothing." This is not to overlook what was said in Chapter 1 about man as created in the image of God. There it was observed that the Genesis story seems to leave room for the concept of *creatio ex nihilo,* but its emphasis is not there. The Genesis story is not concerned with the origin of matter, but with God's creative Word as it brings light into darkness, order out of disorder or cosmos out of chaos. It is against this background that man is set forth in the image of God, man's own continuing work being that of bringing order out of disorder.

Of course, it follows that an alternative to the concept of *creatio ex nihilo* (the view that God in the very beginning did create out of nothing that which is) is the dualistic view that matter and spirit are coeternal. There is no room for this ultimate dualism in monotheistic faith. If God is one God and there is no other, he must antedate all else that is. If this point is pushed, *creatio ex nihilo* may logically follow. Another option is panentheism, today a growing emphasis on the suggestion that God produces the world and man out of his own being. On the other hand, Jewish thinkers backed away from the Oriental idea that matter is evil as well as from the Greek idea that "the nothing" (*to mē on*) which contrasted with the existent was not so much vacancy but untruth.[7] The concept of "nonbeing" barely surfaces in the New Testament, and where it does it may not imply "nothing" but rather potentiality or lack of fulfillment (Rom. 4:17; I Cor. 1:28).

When we come to Paul, we find that in his soteriology he did in some sense build upon the concept of *creatio ex nihilo*. He saw man's salvation as so completely dependent upon God's free grace, God's creative word, and so little dependent upon man's merit or work that nothing short of a view of "creation out of nothing" did justice to his understanding of man's salvation. This comes to forceful expression in Rom. 4:17b, where God is seen as "the one making alive the dead" and calling "the things not being" (*ta mē onta*) "as being" (*hōs onta*).[8] In fact, Paul employs three powerful analogies in this context by which to stress the creative nature of God's saving man. When God saves man it is like his creating something out of nothing, being out of nonbeing (Rom. 4:17b); it is like his bringing Isaac out of the barrenness of Sarah's womb (Rom. 4:19); it is like his raising Jesus from the dead (Rom. 4:24).

In this understanding of creation, Paul stood within Jewish tradition, for there are many traces of it there.[9] The mother of the seven brothers who suffered martyrdom during the Maccabean

revolt encouraged her sons to faithfulness in the face of death
with the assurance that God raises the dead and that God made
the things that are out of that which was not (II Macc. 7:28).
The author of the Syrian Apocalpyse of Baruch addresses God
as "Thou . . . that hast called from the beginning of the world
that which did not yet exist" (II Baruch 21:4) and declares,
"With a word Thou quickenest that which was not" (II Baruch
48:8). Philo wrote of God, "He called the things that are not into
being" (*De specialibus legibus,* IV, 187) and "He brought the
things that were not into being" (*De opificio mundi,* 81).[10]

Paul's portrayal of salvation as *creatio ex nihilo* or as life from
the dead is not confined to Rom. 4:17b. In an earlier letter he
saw the followers of Christ as those whom God had called out:
the "foolish," the "weak," the "classless of the world," the
"nobodies," "the things not being" in order to nullify "the things
being" (I Cor. 1:27 f.). In II Corinthians, God is seen as the one
raising the dead (II Cor. 1:9), as being alone our sufficiency (II
Cor. 3:4–6) ; and Christians are seen as having their treasure in
earthen vessels, dependent upon God who raises the dead (II Cor.
4:7–15), having their strength in their weakness (II Cor. 12:9),
and living in the power of God (II Cor. 13:4). In Colossians (Col.
1:15 ff.) the church is seen as created and sustained by the very
Christ who created all things and in whom all things hold together.
Paul's concern is not with the origin of matter but with the source
of salvation or true existence in salvation.

To conclude, man is made to become, but he becomes only as
he responds to the creative word of God by which he is called.
Creator and Redeemer are one, not rival gods as in Marcionism.
God's intention in creation is brought to fulfillment in redemption. In one sense, salvation is bringing order out of disorder,
cosmos out of chaos. It is God's work of awakening, motivating,
directing, liberating, cleansing, restoring, enabling. This understanding of salvation is reflected in Jesus' description of his saving
work (John 7:23) as "making an entire man well" or, to retain
his play on words, "making a whole (*holon*) man whole (*hygiē*)."

From another perspective, this same salvation is God's creative
work of making something out of nothing, *creatio ex nihilo.* God

saves sinners. Salvation is not reward for man's virtue or works. God does not coerce us into salvation; for any determination would be manipulation and thus damnation rather than salvation (the Achilles' heel of Calvin). But salvation is God's work from beginning to end. It is he who calls, who opens up new possibilities, who forgives, who empowers. We begin to become authentic human beings when we begin to respond to his creative word.

HUMAN AND INHUMAN

To propose that man is "made to become" implies that there is some model or goal for man and that there are norms or standards to govern choice. It presupposes that there is such a thing as being "human" or "inhuman," as right and wrong, as fulfillment or failure. In philosophy and theology this is called "essentialism," i.e., that there is an "essence" somewhere representing the being from which man comes or toward which he moves. But not all accept the idea of "essence." There are existentialists who deny that there is any model or goal and who deny that there are any norms or standards for attaining fulfillment as a human being. Their whole emphasis is upon existence or simply living. All one has is life or existence, a sequence of options with no norms, models, or goals to guide one's choices. To be "human" is simply to exist, whatever the kind of existence one has. Pressed consistently, there could be no such thing as being "inhuman," just different kinds of humanness, whether like Albert Schweitzer or Al Capone, Jesus or Judas.

Although essence and existence, essentialism and existentialism, are philosophical terms and belong to the jargon of philosophy and theology, they do represent concepts that filter down to the common man, whether he is aware of it or not. One does approach life as an essentialist, an existentialist, or with some combination of the two, whether he knows it or not. Consequently, to pursue our Biblical concept of "made to become," we must turn directly to these concepts.

Essential, Existential, or Both?

To speak of "human nature" or even of "being human" implies that there is an "essential" which at least in ideal represents man, a prototype or a goal or an ideal. But this view of man is not universally held. Some thoroughgoing existentialists reject the whole idea that there is a human "essence," especially those who are atheistic (cf. Jean-Paul Sartre, who says that man's "essence" is his existence). Such thoroughgoing existentialism recognizes only that man "exists," that he simply moves from one set of options to another, moving along without a compass and with no harbor toward which to point. Christian existentialists (e.g., Kierkegaard and Marcel) do tend to emphasize essence before existence. Even Heidegger moves from his existentialism to a phenomenology of man and searches for man's essential being, and he can see existence as authentic or inauthentic, a meaningless distinction unless there is an essence. Tillich observes that even the thoroughgoing existentialists actually recognize an essence, as in the case of Freud and Sartre. Freud sees man only in his existential self-estrangement; but he happily is inconsistent, for he also was concerned for therapy. Healing implies some "esse" over against sickness. It implies something which is more human than something else. So also with Sartre. Equating man's "essence" with his existence, Sartre's theory leaves no room for man's being saved or healed, yet Sartre too proves to be happily inconsistent. He calls his existentialism humanism, implying that he has some idea of what man essentially is. Heidegger speaks as if there were no norms for man, so no essential man; yet he speaks of authentic and inauthentic existence. So, the most radical existentialists actually fall back upon essentialism without which they cannot speak.[11]

Essentialism holds to the priority of essence over existence, that there is a "true" humanity which is to be brought to realization in existence. Existentialism affirms the priority of existence over essence, seeing existence as the actualization of essence or even rejecting the very concept of a "true" or essential humanity. Some seek to bridge the gap and to hold to an essentialist-existentialist view.

Essentialism. In philosophy, essence is what a thing is, the permanent and unchanging substance which underlies all outward manifestations. Essence is that in which qualities or attributes inhere. Essentialism assumes a type or archetype, a human essence. When we speak of "human nature" or of being "human," we imply that there is an essentiality, an ideal or goal, which represents true humanity.[12] The very concept of right and wrong implies an essentialist view that somewhere there is the "model" of what it is to be truly human. It is meaningless to say "be a man" unless we mean something specific as to what it is to be a man or to say "be good" unless there is a model of goodness.

Essence is what one is; existence is the fact of being. The essentialist finds the value of man in what he is.[13] The thoroughgoing existentialists find meaning only in the fact of existing. Some affirm the primacy of existence over essence yet find man's value in his essence, in what he is. These may be termed essentialist-existentialists.

Essentialism draws a sharp distinction between two worlds, one called "sensible," the other called "intelligible." The intelligible world is held to consist of "ideas," also known as "essences" or "pure being." This world of ideas may be known by the mind alone, not by the senses. These ideas are understood to be eternal, unchanging, and perfect. Their reality does not depend upon their *existing,* i.e., emerging into phenomena or things such as can be known by the senses, but they may so emerge or exist. These ideas are the models of all things that exist.[14]

Classical philosophy from Plato to the nineteenth century did not question the priority of essence over existence. Theological essentialism, the view which finds essences in God or the transcendental world, may be traced back to Plato, its Christian expression to Augustine. In this view essences are seen to be in some sense divine, if not God himself. Plato held that essence precedes existence and receives nothing from existence. He rejected the idea that existence gives essence its actual being, thus enriching it. Rather, he saw existence as reducing or impoverishing essence. Essence is not fully realized in existence. For example: no one tree brings to actualization all that is meant by "tree." In passing from the potential to the actual, essence is diminished. For example, to make one choice out of many options is to narrow down potentiality from many possibilities to one actuality.

To Plato, the existences belonging to the sensible world have only a restricted kind of being. The very fact that they *become* reflects their change and reduction. Their fact of becoming is but a step in the direction on nonexistence. The flower before us today was not here yesterday and will be gone tomorrow. The beauty of a given flower exists today but beauty itself belongs to the permanence of essence and not to the flux of existence. Beauty varies from flower to flower and no flower is the embodiment of beauty in its fullness or perfection. Only essences have being without any admixture of nonbeing. Only they are immutable, eternal, necessary. By contrast, the phenomena of the world which seem to be so real to the senses are in fact only existences which have no real being. These seemingly real existences are only passing shadows of the essences. Just as the shadow is wholly dependent upon the reality which casts it, so all existences are dependent upon the essences which they only in part actualize.

Also, the value given to the existent presupposes the essential, whether the value be moral, aesthetic, or otherwise. To say that a flower is beautiful presupposes some norm of beauty. To say that one is good or that he is human implies that there is a norm of goodness or humanity. As Foulquié sums it up, "Every judgment passed on an existent being presupposes that we know its essence." [15]

Applied to man, Plato's essentialism found man's essence in the "soul" which he saw to preexist in the intelligible world before it came into union with a body. In its bodily state it has some memory of its previous state where it belonged to the world of ideas or essences. This view is opposed to the Judeo-Christian view that man was created from the dust of the earth and that into his bodily existence came the breath of God which transformed him into "a living soul" (Gen. 2:7).

What Plato's essentialism knows as "existence" is in some sense parallel to what in Biblical theology is known as the "Fall," but there is a fundamental difference. To Plato the "fall" (not his term) of essence into existence was one of reduction, impoverishment, the limitation belonging to finitude. All theology that sees salvation as redemption from creation bears more similarity to Plato than to Scripture.

In Biblical perspective man's *existence* is not his "fall." Existence in time and space, in the world, in bodily form made from the dust of the earth, is the gift of God's creative work. Man's "fall" is a *moral* problem (cf. Rom. 1:18, 28; 3:10–18; and *passim*). Man's problem is not that his "essence" has emerged into "existence." His problem is not in his finitude or his being caught in time and space. Man's problem is that he has abused his freedom, cutting himself off from the "eternal life" which belongs first to God and which God offers man.

Consequently, salvation for man is not deliverance from his finitude or creatureliness. It is rather the overcoming of his moral problem of rebellion and failure, as well as his restoration to the fellowship of God, where he is given eternal life (John 17:3). The "eternal life" which was "with the Father" has so penetrated our existential world of the senses that it has been "heard," "looked upon" with eyes, and "touched" with hands (I John 1:1–3). We may even now participate in that life. Essence and existence are open to one another.

Man may thus be seen as bipolar, on the horizon of two worlds, situated in the world of existences and participating in the world of essences. It is only because there is a world of essences, where there is a being without limit or fault and because he has some participation in that world that he can know that in his existence there is limit and fault. It is proper, then, to speak of "being human" or "becoming human." It does make sense to affirm that man is "made to become." This is one of the polarities of our existence.

Existentialism. The term "existential" is used in both a popular and a philosophical sense. In popular usage, it stands for involvement. To experience something existentially is to participate personally as opposed to being a mere spectator. To read about a fire may leave one uninvolved. To awaken in the night to find one's own house afire is existential. In the more philosophical sense, existentialism is the view that existence has priority over essence. In its radical form only existence is acknowledged. All thought of a model or an ideal man is rejected. Man is seen only in process, without model or goal. One simply moves from one set of options to another, each option exercised determining the new set of options.

Existentialism is concerned not with existence in general but existence in particular, e.g., my existence or your existence. Existence is an act, a becoming. It is the movement by choice from possibility to reality. Existence presupposes choice, and choice presupposes liberty. Existence thus belongs to persons, not to things. Only man chooses to be or become himself. It is proper to encourage another to "be a man" or to ask a child what he intends to be when he grows up. One would not ask that of a puppy. He will be a dog, but not by choice; and he will not know what he is.

Freedom belongs necessarily to personal existence, to one's choice to become. That there are limits to this freedom is acknowledged. What the possibilities are for existence depends in part on genetics and in part on environment. One born white has no option of becoming black. One with a small, frail body cannot become the heavyweight boxing champion of the world. And one cannot completely escape his cultural impingements. But one does have some freedom in what he makes of his gifts and limitations. He has some freedom in his attitudes, in his values, and in what he permits to be done to himself. He may have no choice as to whether another runs over him or not, but he has some choice as to whether he is moved to anger, hate, or hostility.

There is a more basic limitation to all freedom. There is the freedom to choose, but there is not the freedom not to choose, for "not to choose, in fact, is to choose not to choose." [16] One cannot escape choosing. One may choose among options, but he cannot escape making some choice. There is a sense in which man is "condemned to be free." [17] Life for man is a sequence of choices. But at the deepest level there is no freedom behind the act of choosing. One must choose. It is not only that we had no option in our being brought into the world, but we have no escape from choosing whether or not to bring others into the world. Opponents of birth control, e.g., contend that one has no right to deny birth to another. One could ask if he has the right to choose life for another. One may choose to give life or not to give life but he cannot choose not to choose. He may protest that he does not want the freedom or responsibility for making that choice, but he cannot escape this "dreadful freedom." He is indeed "condemned to be free," but it is a freedom as to *what* to choose, not *whether* to choose. Logic would push this back to God himself. He could choose to create or choose not to create, but he could not choose to dispense with choice. Is this something of the "cross" inherent in existence, in being free, in being personal?

For the consistent existentialist, the anguish of choice is yet greater. Not only must he choose but he must choose with no norm or standard by which to choose. He has no principle by which to judge the soundness of the choice, whether well or ill. For example: in Sartre, to exist is to become oneself, to become a particular person. One is born "man" as regards species, but one must choose what individual person he is to become. For Sartre there is no divine or other essence to impose itself upon a person. Existence remains open—upon nothing.

THE POLARITY OF ESSENCE AND EXISTENCE

It seems to this writer that in Biblical perspective man is to be seen in the tension or polarity between essence and existence. Man is created for freedom and with decision as both a privilege and a necessity. At the same time he is created in the image of

God (Gen. 1:26 f.). There is a model for man as well as a goal. He is not a ship at sea without compass or harbor. His origin is in God and his destiny is life in fellowship with God. Man is moral—i.e., he lives under moral, ethical, personal claims and demands. He has a deep-seated conscience (Rom. 2:15), a sense of right and wrong. On the side of his freedom is the power to choose what kind of person he is to become (Josh. 24:15). But he chooses as one who finds himself continually addressed and called to decision.[18]

God Is and God Exists. That a Christian existentialism is not an anomaly may be argued first from the Biblical view of God. God is and God exists. God has essence and existence. Of course it is a faith affirmation to say that God is, that eternally he is. That God exists is also a faith affirmation, but it is a reality to which man has more immediate access. God is known to faith as one who is encountered. He is known as a presence.[19] This is not something subject to "proof," least of all something which one person can prove to another person. However, it is for countless people an unshakable assurance as they sense in their lives the very kind of presence attested to in Scripture. "I am the Alpha and the Omega, says the Lord God, who is and who was and who is to come, the Almighty" (Rev. 1:8).

God is known in Scripture as "the God of Abraham, and the God of Isaac, and the God of Jacob" (cf. Ex. 3:6, 15, 16; Matt. 22:32; Mark 12:26; Luke 20:37). He is not known in Scripture in abstract terms, e.g., as the "unmoved mover." Neither is he described in such abstract terms as omnipotent, omniscient, omnipresent, although these are apparent implications from the way God is addressed or referred to in Scripture. "Person" may not be an adequate term for God, but it is the best man has. God is thought of in personal terms. Moreover, he is seen as an existent being, as having not only being but existence. He acts, he feels, he speaks, he judges, he comforts, he loves, and he lives. The incarnation implies both essence and existence: "In the beginning *was* the Word, and the Word was with God, and the Word was God. . . . And the Word *became* flesh and dwelt among us" (John 1:1, 14; italics added).

The three great themes of creation, revelation, and redemption all contemplate God as a being who exists. He is not a static essence but a dynamic being who decides among options, who acts, and who relates (Ex. 3:13–22). He is the creator of all that is (Gen. 1:1, 27; 2:7). He takes the initiative to make himself knowable (Rom. 1:19–20). He penetrates history and human existence to redeem man from all that distorts, or degrades, or defeats man (I John 1:1–4).

The strongest existentialist affirmation about God is the incarnation: "The Word became flesh and tabernacled among us" (John 1:14). This is the view that God himself was uniquely present in the historical, bodily existence of Jesus of Nazareth. God had spoken in various manners and measures through his prophets, but in the age which is the culmination of all the ages he has spoken in his Son (Heb. 1:1–4). God had been coming to his people in various ways, but ultimately he came in Jesus of Nazareth (Isa. 40:3; Matt. 3:3). God came into history and into bodily existence so tangibly that he could be heard, seen, and touched (I John 1:1–3).

Man Is and Must Become. Man, too, is to be seen in the polarity of essence and existence. Man is made to become. There is a model. It is proper to speak of being "human" or "inhuman." This model came to full existential reality in the Man Christ Jesus. What man was made to become, Jesus proved to be (Heb. 2:6–9). Jesus Christ is more than example, but he is that (I Peter 2:21). There is that which God requires of man (cf. Micah 6:8; Mark 12:29 f.). There is the concept of a full-grown man, finding his fullness in Christ (Eph. 4:13). There is an essence or being for man. Käsemann correctly sees man as "a being who cannot be determined solely in the light of his own self. His existence stems from outside himself." [20] Man's being and existence depend upon God's grace: "It is no longer I who live, but Christ lives in me" (Gal. 2:20).

Man is also existential, obviously so. He is called constantly to decision. He is a pilgrim on the way; he has not arrived. His true being or authentic existence is a goal before him. In this sense his existence precedes his essence, but it is an existence moving toward an essence which does have shape. There are norms by which he is to be guided as he moves through existential choices toward his ultimate essence—he is a child of God now and ultimately will be like Christ (I John 3:1–3). He is to be "poor in spirit" and not arrogant; he is to grieve over wrong; he is to be gentle; he is to hunger and thirst for righteousness; he is to be merciful; he is to be cleansed in heart; he is to be a peacemaker (Matt. 5:3–9). Man is to be characterized by love, joy, peace, patience, kindness, goodness, faith and fidelity, gentleness, and self-control (Gal. 5:22).

Man is made to become. He is thrust into a freedom in which he chooses the kind of self he becomes. Man is not made to be a thing determined, an automat to be operated. He is not intended to be a xerox copy or to live by proxy. Käsemann aptly observes that God does not want stereotypes who let themselves be fitted into patterns and programs, but that man is to resist uniformity, finding his own proper station in life.[21]

SALVATION IN THREE DIMENSIONS

Salvation is not simply a state but rather an endless path thrown open to us, an experience of being divinely addressed and called to pilgrimage.[22] Man is continually being called and challenged to be "a new creation and a new man." [23] Salvation is a possibility through divine calling, but it is never a divine determination, for man can hear or close his ears, obey or disobey (Matt. 23:37; Rom. 10:21). Man can also respond (John 1:12). The divine calling is out of divine freedom, and the human response is out of divinely given freedom to respond or not. Salvation has a beginning at the point of one's basic commitment to the divine calling; it has an ultimate goal which is to be realized only in the redemption of the body beyond death; it is between this beginning and this goal a pilgrimage.[24]

Salvation as Past. In the medical world a "crisis" experience is that point at which an illness is arrested and the patient who has been moving toward death begins to move toward life. To a layman visiting in the ward of a hospital there may be no apparent difference between the health of one man and that of another man on the adjacent bed. They have the same temperature, the same coloring, and the same body strength. But to the attending physician there is a most significant difference. One man is dying and the other is recovering. The difference is not in condition but in direction. One is responding to medication or surgery and the other is not. So it is with salvation. There is a "crisis" experience, a point at which the direction of a life is changed or a point at which a life begins to be open to the resources which can give it fulfillment. Thus the gospel begins with a call to repentance (*metanoia* as conversion) and faith, new life ordered under the kingdom of God (Mark 1:1–4; Matt. 3:1–3).

This is not to say that every "crisis" experience in salvation must be traumatic or dramatic. It is not to be expected that the turning of a little child to God's calling will be marked by deep grief, contrition, and struggle. There is no long life of rebellion from which to repent. There may be the glad response of one who yields to God's calling as he hears it (Mark 12:37). For one whose life has been one of stubborn resistance or shameful degradation a traumatic crisis is to be expected, as with the psalmist who cried out for mercy and cleansing (Ps. 51). But whether traumatic or quiet and barely perceptible, there is a beginning point for conscious, free response to God's calling.

In New Testament terms, this beginning of salvation is at the point of submission to the kingdom of God, i.e., the sovereign rule of God as it confronts us in his anointed, the Christ (cf. Matt. 3:2; Mark 1:4, 14 f.). The kingdom of God is the rule of God. It stands for the claim upon us which is ultimate and absolute. It is the claim which overrides all other claims, even that of one's family, one's country, or one's own self. Of course, this ultimate claim is not incompatible with the proper claims of family, state, or self. It is only when family, state, or self seeks to be "God," itself making ultimate claims, that its claims are incompatible with God's claims as well as with man's own fulfillment. To New Testament faith, God's kingdom confronts man and addresses man in the one whom God has anointed to rule, his Christ ("Messiah" in Hebrew and "Christ" in Greek mean "anointed").

The polarity of essence and existence is reflected in this call to repentance, this call to a turning to God in whom man finds the ultimate claim under which he finds his true existence. That there is a claim from without says that man is more than what is acknowledged in thoroughgoing existentialism. Man is not a ship without compass or harbor. Man is addressed and called to decision in which he chooses the kind of existence he is to have. But his existence depends upon something or someone outside himself. The God who *is* calls man to the decision in which man *becomes* or begins to become. Man is called to become man, nothing more and nothing less. He is called to become himself, himself and none other. This is the beginning of salvation.

In various ways, through various models, the New Testament affirms the radical difference between "those who are perishing" and "those who are being saved" (I Cor. 1:18) as well as the radical discontinuity between the self from which and the self to which one is being saved. Jesus taught that we must "turn and become as little children" if we are to enter the kingdom of heaven (Matt. 18:3). The Gospel of John recognizes that one must *become* a child of God, and the right or power to become a child of God is a divinely given privilege (John 1:12 f.). The necessity for and divine origin of this new kind of existence is forcefully presented in the conversation between Jesus and Nicodemus under the analogy of being "begotten from above" (see also I Peter 1:3; James 1:18, 21). To have a new destiny man must have a new origin, a new whence if a new whither.[25]

To truly *be,* man must *become;* and his new beginning must be from God. God is; man becomes. Jesus could say, "Before Abraham became, I am" (John 8:58). This is a deliberate use of the Old Testament "I am," the self-designation of $JHWH$ (Ex. 3:14). Jesus *came* that man might have life in abundance (John 10:10). The new and abundant life which man needs is precisely "the life eternal which was with the Father" and which penetrated history and flesh so deeply and tangibly in the person of Jesus Christ that men could see it with their own eyes, hear it with their own ears, and feel it with their own hands (I John 1:1–3). The purpose of God's redemptive thrust is that man may have a new beginning as he enters into fellowship (*koinōnia*) with "the Father and with his Son Jesus Christ" (I John 1:3).

Paul forcefully employs the model of a new creation in setting forth the origin, nature, and purpose of our salvation: "If anyone is in Christ, there is a new creation. Old things have passed away and look, new things have come to be!" (II Cor. 5:17). Salvation is seen as a new existence, divine in origin and being brought into conformity with a specific goal. Existence is not the uncharted course of a ship without compass or port. It is the beginning of a new existence being made into the righteousness of God (II Cor. 5:21); and it is the conversion of the egocentric into one who lives not unto himself but unto the Christ who gave himself (II Cor. 5:15).

To the same end, Paul also employs the model of death and resurrection. One for whom salvation has begun is one who has "died" with Christ and begun to live with him (Gal. 2:19–20; II Cor. 5:14 f.). Where salvation has begun, "the old man" has been crucified with Christ and the new man has been raised up in his place (Rom. 6:4–6). One thus has become a child who can say "Abba" (Father) to God (Rom. 8:15 f.). Those who were "no people" have become God's people (Rom. 9:25; cf. Hos. 2:23). The man with true righteousness is the one who by faith lives out of the faithfulness of God (Rom. 1:17; Gal. 3:11; Heb. 10:38; cf. Hebrew text of Hab. 2:4).

The radical disjunctive between the "old" man and the "new" is both a decisive act and a continuing one, for the Christian is to be one "having put on the new man, being renewed unto knowledge according to the image of the one having created him" (Col. 3:10). There is, then, an "essence" from which man is "created" and toward which he is brought in redemption.

As seen in Chapter 1, Hebrews responds to the question raised in Ps. 8, with special attention to the gap between the promised glory of man and his actual existence (Heb. 2:5–18). Man's promised destiny and glory is first fulfilled in Jesus Christ, brought to his "glory and honor": only through "suffering and death" (Heb. 2:8 f.). It is only in and through Jesus Christ that man is brought to his own destiny (Heb. 2:10). Savior and saved are out of the same One, and the saved are acknowledged as the Savior's brothers (Heb. 2:10–12). Through suffering he becomes the enabler of a new existence to those who obey (Heb. 5:8–10). As the "forerunner," Jesus leads the way into the Holy of Holies, the presence of God, where man becomes truly man (Heb. 6:19–20). He saves us by writing a new law in our hearts (Heb. 10:16). He makes a "fresh and living way" to God (Heb. 10:19 f.), and he is the "pioneer and perfecter" of our faith (Heb. 12:2). Thus through various models, colorful and powerful, the writer of Hebrews shows Christ's work to be that of enabling man *to become* in God's presence what man was made *to be*.

Salvation as Present Process. Paul distinguished sharply between those who are "being destroyed" and those who are "being saved" (I Cor. 1:18). This is to view both destruction (being lost) and salvation in dynamic rather than static terms. Being "lost" is not a matter of being at a certain stage of bondage, corruption, or misdirection. It is to be moving in the wrong direction. It is to be moving away from God rather than toward him. It is to be moving away from one's own authentic existence rather than toward it. Likewise, salvation is not a static matter, a certain condition or state. It is a new relationship, a new direction, a new openness to God, to others, to things, to self, an openness which admits into one's life the resources for true being and existence. In Paul's language, one is either "being destroyed" or "being saved."

The analogies of "destroyed" and "saved" are not to be literalized. They are to be taken more seriously than literally. One is not "lost" in the sense that his location is not known. He can be "lost" in full view of everyone. To be "lost" is to miss one's authentic being and existence. To be "saved" is to be brought into authentic being and existence. To be "destroyed" is not to be annihilated. A watch is basically a timepiece. It is "lost" as a timepiece when it won't keep time. It is not that one does not know where the watch is, but that it does not fulfill its purpose. One may smash a watch with a hammer and thus "destroy" it.

He has not annihilated it, for the pieces are still there. He has "destroyed" it as a timepiece and as such it is "lost." Man is never annihilated; he may be "destroyed" or "lost" as a person. On the other hand, he may be "saved." To be saved is not to become God; it is not to become an angel; it is not to become a fraction, as a Gnostic "soul" or ascetic "saint." It is to become a man—nothing less and nothing more. It is to become a particular man, oneself—that one and no other. There is a beginning to this salvation and an ultimate goal, but between beginning and goal is a life of "being saved."

Seen in its present dimension, salvation is not so much a state as a journey, a pilgrimage. It is "an endless path which has been thrown open to us" who now stand under "the sign of exodus" and whose "horizon is hope." [26] Paul saw it as a race in which one forgets what is in the past and strains toward the goal ahead (Phil. 3:13 f.). He explicitly rejects any notion of salvation as known already in its fullness (Phil. 3:12 f.). John, too, looked beyond the present for completion, finding the present to be meaningful yet short of the ultimate goal: we are children of God now but what we shall be is yet to be disclosed! (I John 3:2). Salvation is neither a romantic "journey into adventure" nor a nihilist "march into no-man's-land," but it does contain "unplumbed depths of its future" (cf. Gen., ch. 12; Heb., ch. 12).[27]

Salvation as Future. Anticipating the coming of Christ, Paul declared that "now is our salvation nearer than when we believed" (Rom. 13:11). Apparently thinking of the parousia, Paul called for a putting away of the "works of darkness" and a putting on of "the weapons of light" (Rom. 13:12). He called for a life appropriate to ones who put on the Lord Jesus Christ (Rom. 13:13 f.). It is clear that Paul here sees the Christian life as progressive, moving from "darkness" to "light," and also as having a fixed goal in the future, the coming of Christ.

In its completion, Paul saw salvation as including "the redemption of our body" (Rom. 8:23) and apparently also the redemption of creation itself (Rom. 8:18–22). This is congenial with the holistic view of Scripture, where man is seen not as a Greek "soul" caught in a body but rather as belonging properly to the created order as well as to God the Creator. Man is himself only in his bodily existence, and body too is to be redeemed. Salvation at no point, whether past, present, or future, is indifferent to man's body. The whole bodily self is to be under redemption at every stage. In this life, one is to "glorify God" in his body (I Cor. 6:20), for the body is "the temple" of the Holy Spirit (I Cor. 6:19). One is to present his body "a living sacrifice, holy and well-pleasing to God" (Rom. 12:1). The body is not a lower self to be despised or rejected. It is an essential aspect of a holistic self.

Ultimately the body is to be redeemed through resurrection. This means its deliverance from corruptibility and weakness (I Cor. 15:35–58). What is now a "natural body" will be raised as a "spiritual body" (I Cor. 15:44). What precisely this means remains a mystery, but it is clear that it will be a real body, whatever the change in its nature. There will be some continuity between "the body sown" and "the body raised," just as there is some continuity between the seed planted and the new plant which springs from it (I Cor. 15:37). There will be both continuity and discontinuity, the same recognizable body yet freed from decay and death.

Although he does not pursue the subject, Paul indicates that "the creation" itself will be redeemed (Rom. 8:21). This redemption of the creation will parallel that of the body. Man's existence in a body and in the world is not seen, as with Greeks and others, as a fall into the material or into finiteness from which it is to be redeemed. Rather, man is seen as belonging properly to bodily existence and creation both in his own creation and in his own redemption.

This view of salvation brings under judgment any despising of the body through ascetic reduction or libertine indulgence. The body is to be neither despised nor worshiped, neither denied nor licensed. The body is to find fulfillment as a part of the wholeness of man relating properly to the claims of God, the claims of mankind, the claims of the wholeness of the individual person, and the claims of the world about one. Also, this view of salvation brings under judgment all despising of the natural order, either through pollution, depletion, or other abuse. Nature is neither to be despised nor worshiped. Its proper place under God and in relation to man is to be seen and affirmed. Body and all creation have meaning now. They are to be under redemption now, and they await their final and full redemption at Christ's coming.

OK YET NOT OK

The book *I'm OK—You're OK* has had considerable influence in church circles and in preaching.[28] It brings into focus an important truth and is a needed corrective to much misunderstanding of personal selfhood. The theme does not embody the whole truth, however, and needs to be kept in balance. The truth with which it is concerned can best be stated in paradox: "OK yet not OK."

The undeniable and all important truth of the book is that each person has worth as the gift of God's grace. One does not have to earn the right to acceptance. The wonder of God's love is that while we were yet sinners God loved us and gave his best for us (Rom. 5:7 f.). Our achievement culture has greatly falsified human worth and caused untold damage. The popular idea that one has worth only as he "makes something of himself" is false. Much damage is done in the implications of the warning, "If you are ever going to amount to anything!" This implies that one does not amount to anything now. In Biblical perspective, value is given to each person in the very act of creation. Each is of infinite worth. There is a real sense in which "I'm OK and you're OK." We do not have to earn acceptance.

But the very love which accepts another person refuses to accept the things which limit, misdirect, distort, deplete, or otherwise rob another of fulfillment. A physician accepts a patient as he is. He does not say, "Come back when you are better." But the very fact that he is a person of worth even in his sickness means that he is worth all that is required for healing. So with love always. It accepts the beloved, however lacking the beloved may

be. But at the same time love seeks the other's maximum enhancement.

We are made to become. We are to see value in ourselves and
in others as we are, and this means immediate and unconditional
acceptance of ourselves and of one another. But the love which
says "OK" must also say "not OK." Fulfillment in terms of the
being and existence which might be must ever be love's goal.
Love sees one as he is and accepts him as a person of value. Love
sees what one might be and says, "Why not?"

No one has said it better than Tillich: "One could say that
the courage to be is the courage to accept oneself as accepted in
spite of being unacceptable." [29] Tillich went on to say: "The healing helper who tried to convince his patient that he was not really
guilty would do him a great disservice. He would prevent him
from taking his guilt into his self-affirmation." [30]

Implications for Education

In his essay "A Theology of Education," Tillich cogently analyzed three basic concepts of education,[31] and these options remain before us today. Education may be technical training,
induction, or humanistic or some combination of these three
approaches. While the first two are inescapable and proper within
limits, the third is the one most congenial to the position taken
in this chapter, that persons are "made to become."

Training is the most elementary level of education. It has a
proper place, even an indispensable one. A child is trained from
birth in the basics of eating, drinking, bodily function, speech,
etc. Further along, one is trained to ride a tricycle, a bicycle, or
a motorcycle. His fingers are trained to function automatically
at the keyboard of a typewriter or piano. The mind is trained to
recite or apply the multiplication tables. From birth into adult
life one is trained in many ways, but this is not the real test of
personhood. The lower animals can also be trained: to work under
a saddle or in harness, to "point" birds, to jump through a hoop,

or to ride a bicycle. Some animals excel us in aptitude for training. This surely is not the ultimate in the education of a person.

A second level of education is induction. There is a proper place for inducting another into one's values, knowledge, principles, or ideals. In fact, this is inescapable in human relationships. Whether we do it consciously or not, we do influence one another in such terms. Even if one sets out deliberately to avoid inducting another into his values and ways, he cannot completely escape it. A child by contagion catches something of the fears, biases, prejudices, hopes, mores, and ideals of those about him. But not only is induction inescapable; it is valid within certain limits. There is even an obligation to offer another person what one sincerely believes to be true or to enhance personal existence.

Even in matters of religion, one may properly offer another his beliefs, values, and hopes. What is not proper is coercion. To describe to another and even to seek to persuade another to the faith by which one lives is right. To "brainwash," to intimidate, to manipulate, or in any way to coerce is evil. Yet worse is the attempt to impose upon another what one does not really believe for himself. This is the shameful wrong inherent in any pledge forced upon "mixed marriages," where one partner to a marriage is required to bring up any child born to the union in the religious faith of the spouse. This is to require a child to accept what the parent himself rejects. This is fraud. It is the shame of anyone who requires it of another or who submits to such religious blackmail. It is a crime against the victimized child.

God himself does not compel faith. He instructs, warns, and pleads, but he does not compel. It is no mark of the children of God to seek to force others into a faith they do not freely choose. It is proper to "train up a child in the way he should go" (Prov. 22:6), but it is not right to reduce him to a thing to be manipulated, an animal to be trained, or a slave to be commanded. It was in part against the temptation of the zealous to impose "that which is holy" or their "pearls" upon unwilling recipients that Jesus gave stern warning in the Sermon on the Mount (Matt. 7:6).

Tillich's third and highest level of education he called humanistic.[32] By this he meant the awakening of another into authentic, growing personhood. It has been said that a true teacher can have no disciples. One is most successful as a teacher when his students become his peers, his colleagues. The teacher is most successful when he so relates to his students that he is no longer needed as a teacher. It is education at its highest level when one begins to function as a mature person, authentically feeling, thinking, choosing, living. Jesus committed himself to making us not his "slaves" but his trusted, responsible "friends" (John 15:14–17).

If those who are made are to have their maximum opportunity to become, it is necessary that in the home, in the schools, in the churches, and elsewhere we keep in proper perspective and proportion the training, induction, and evolutionary aspects of education. This is wisdom for parents, for schoolteachers, for church workers, and for all of us in all human relationships. Personages we can manufacture. Persons must grow. It is our proper function to provide for ourselves and for one another the soil and the atmosphere most congenial to growth as persons—made to become!

Chapter 5

FREE
YET BOUND

Man under salvation is free yet bound, bound yet free. "For freedom Christ freed us!" (Gal. 5:1). "Blessed be the Lord God of Israel for he visited and made redemption [*lutrōsis*—i.e., freedom] for his people" (Luke 1:68). Abiding in his word one becomes in reality his disciple and thus "ye shall know the truth, and the truth [*alētheia*—i.e., reality] shall make you free" (John 8:31 f.). "If the Son shall make you free, you shall be free indeed!" (John 8:36).

Man is called to freedom, but it is a freedom under the kingdom or rule of God. Man's truest freedom is life lived under claims which are intrinsic to his nature, not arbitrary or artificial. The primary claim under which man becomes truly himself is the ultimate and absolute claim which God, his creator and redeemer, has upon him. Closely allied with this ultimate claim are the claims of his fellowman upon him and the claims which he has upon himself. Man's freedom is not that of an island but that which he has in relationship with God, with others, with himself, and even with the total ecological situation in which he exists, his larger house which includes his bodily existence and his total historical existence in God's larger world. This polarity of freedom and bondage cannot escape its paradoxical nature, the tension in which authentic existence becomes possible.

Freedom implies freedom from and freedom for. One is free

to the extent that he is able to become a true human being, nothing more and nothing less. This means freedom from all which prevents fulfillment as a human being. When is a bird free? Is it not free when it is able to fly, to sing, to nest, to migrate? When is a drilling bit free? Is it not free when it is able to function as a drilling bit? But a bit is bound at the very time it is free. Being a part of a larger tool is a part of its fulfillment, its freedom to be a drilling bit. For us to be free does not mean independence from all that is not oneself. We are free when our relationship with God, other people, all aspects of self, and our total situation is such that we can emerge and function as authentic persons.

One may naïvely think that to be free is to be without dependence upon or obligation to any other. The "prodigal" son probably sought freedom in seeking to separate himself from his father's home (Luke 15:11–24). Out there in the far country he would be free—to come and to go, to be himself, to answer to no one. But what an illusion and how sobering his ultimate disillusionment! Separated from family he was not free but frustrated, limited, defeated. He first found freedom as a son and as a person when he offered himself back to his home. One cannot be free alone for the simple reason that one cannot be oneself alone (see Chapter 3). Only in God's presence and in the presence of other persons can one begin to become himself, and thus to be free. Free to be me. Free to be you. Only as we are bound to one another are we free.

THE PARADOX OF SLAVERY AND FREEDOM

Jesus said, "No longer do I call you slaves. . . . I have called you friends" (John 15:15). Paul and other early Christians called themselves "slaves" of Christ (cf. Rom. 1:1; Phil. 1:1; Titus 1:1; James 1:1; I Peter 2:16; II Peter 1:1; Jude 1). The paradox remains. Ours is a paradoxical freedom, a paradoxical servitude.[1] True freedom for man is found in surrendering freedom to God. When Adam tried to snatch absolute freedom and sovereignty, he lost his freedom (Gen. 3:1–7). John the Baptist and

Jesus announced the kingdom of God (God's sovereign rule; God as king) and called men to submit unconditionally to that sovereign claim (Matt. 3:1 f.; Mark 1:14 f.). Just as one lives only by dying (John 12:24 f.), gains life only by losing it (Mark 8:35), is exalted by humbling himself (Luke 14:11), is first only by becoming last (Mark 10:31), so one becomes a free man only by becoming a willing slave to God. The meek are those to whom the kingdom of God is given (Luke 12:32).

Jesus rejected the status of slaves for his people and offered them the dignity of friends (John 15:15). He indicated that the essence of slavery is to work without meaning. The slave does not know what his master is doing. The slave only performs. He does not share in the plans and purposes nor in the fruits of his work. The expression "work like a slave" is misleading. Usually it implies that slavery consists of hard work. But the essence of slavery is not the hardness of work but the meaninglessness of it. No slave can be driven to work as hard as a free man chooses to work when impelled by a great motive. It is when work is meaningless that it is toil and tedium. God did not offer "paradise" as a place of leisure alone. It was a garden to be kept (Gen. 2:8–15). Work was a provision before Adam sinned, not a curse imposed as penalty for sin. Work is the privilege of sharing creatively with God. Jesus said, "My Father works until now, and I also work" (John 5:17). He also said, "It is necessary for us to work the works of the one who sent me, while it is day; the night comes when no one is able to work" (John 9:4). But in admitting us into his confidence, in letting us know him and his purposes, Jesus lifts us to the status of friends; we are not really slaves (John 15:14 f.).

Paul saw the paradox of freedom and slavery and applied it to situations in the Roman Empire where some had the legal status of slaves and some that of freemen. He assured the one who had the legal status of a slave that in Christ he was in fact the Lord's freedman! He also reminded the one who legally was free that he belonged to the Lord and was a "slave of Christ" (I Cor. 7:22). The New Testament does not know Christ as Savior alone; he must be Lord if he is to be Savior. But it is precisely in this "bondage" that one is free. In Christ one is freed from "the oldness of the letter" so that he may "serve in newness of spirit" (Rom. 7:6). One need not be a legalist, striving to achieve some external standard. He may know the joyous freedom of one who has been accepted into the family of God and who may live creatively with God. As "slaves of the Lord" (Rom. 12:11) or "of Christ" (Rom. 14:18) we may "through love serve one another" (Gal. 5:13). This is to serve the gospel (Phil. 2:22) and to serve righteousness (Rom. 6:19).

The bondage which is most serious is not that imposed from without. Slavery is not condoned in the New Testament, although the best that many could do was to transcend it (I Cor. 7:22). Where one did have opportunity to escape legal slavery, he was encouraged to make the most of the opportunity (I Cor. 7:21). But the slavery most to be feared was of another sort. It was slavery to fear (Rom. 8:15), slavery to corruption (Rom. 8:21), slavery to the fear of death (Heb. 2:15), slavery to mammon, or hoarded wealth (Matt. 6:24), slavery to sin (Rom. 6:6, 20; John 8:34), slavery to false gods (Gal. 4:8 f.). The alternative to all such bondage is the kingdom of God (Matt. 6:33). Under God's rule one is free indeed.

A further word may be said regarding another aspect of the paradox of freedom and bondage. It may be said that one's faith gives him his freedom; one's love places limits on that freedom. For example, faith frees one from the arbitrary, superficial restrictions of legalism. Paul's faith freed him to eat whatever was set before him, giving thanks to God for it (I Cor. 10:25-27, 30 f.). His love prompted him who was "free from all" to bring himself "under bondage to all" (I Cor. 9:19). Since love's concern is to build up the other (I Cor. 8:1), it is willing to relinquish personal rights wherever so doing can serve the needs of others. This does not mean that love always yields. Sometimes it can serve only by exposing and rejecting another's scruples, but its disposition is never to assert selfishly its own rights but to liberate and edify the other. Thus faith frees, and love in a sense binds.

FREEDOM AND OBLIGATION

Man's basic "bondage" is that of his own conscience, his sense of moral obligation. Should he be able to throw off every other restraint, he still has himself to live with. Paradoxically, he is freest to be himself, an authentic person, precisely when he lives by this most enlightened and respected conscience. He is most nearly "dead" when he has so thwarted, bludgeoned, and blinded his conscience that "his heart is darkened" and he can no longer distinguish Creator from creature (Rom. 1:21–23). Freedom and the "bondage" of conscience do belong together in personal fulfillment.

It was precisely at this point of the recognition of individual accountability that man in the Old Testament emerged in conscious individuality. Eichrodt states it well:

> The basic phenomenon peculiar to man is the consciousness of responsibility. In primitive man this is chiefly expressed as collective responsibility, in which the consciousness of the I remains uncertain and weakly developed. Only when responsibility breaks through the collective constraint and releases the individual from his circle, making him rely upon himself as a responsible individual, is it possible for full personal consciousness to awaken.[2]

Man's sense of responsibility, his deep consciousness that he is answerable to God first and last (cf. Ps. 51:4), his awareness that he lives under the direct claim of God's "Thou shalt" or "Thou shalt not," is not unrelieved bondage. Ultimately, it is not bondage at all. It is man's freedom. Ancient Israel knew that God's demands and commands had come in the context of merciful provision and care. In Israel's history under God, "the divine Lawgiver was recognized from the beginning as the divine Lifegiver, and his demand was distinguished from all arbitrary tyranny as a call to a relation of grace."[3] Torah was far more than command; it was primarily teaching, the self-revelation of God and the disclosure to man of man's own true nature. Again, Eichrodt is to the point:

And the individual's obligation, in the "Thou shalt" of the Law, received from the relation of grace an inner motivation and illumination in virtue of which it was seen, not as a heavy yoke, but as a necessary and blessed form of life, as a liberation from chaotic self-destruction.[4]

Unless he finds his existence under God's loving claim, man will self-destruct.

Saul, the son of Kish, sought to substitute ritual sacrifice for obedience to God, and in so doing he learned what it is to be self-destroyed. Samuel, the prophet, pointed not only to the obedience which is better than ritual sacrifice, but also showed that the price of disobedience was Saul's loss of identity or freedom to become the king he was designed to be (I Sam. 15:22 f.). Because of willful disobedience to God, Saul was denied the right to be king. Through disobedience to God we fail to become.

Man finds his freedom in obedience to God. It is not in conformity to community mores or to the external and often arbitrary and superficial demands of some religious establishment that man fulfills his obligation to God and finds his freedom. It is as man hears God's call, "Repent!" or "Turn!" (*shubu* in Hebrew; *metanoeite* in Greek), that he is compelled to make his own judgment and decision. Nothing short of this satisfies God's claim. Nothing short of this opens the way to man's freedom and fulfillment.

GENETIC BONDAGE AND FREEDOM

A strong case can be made from genetics that man is not free and cannot be free. Some conclude that man is wholly determined by genetics: his racial identity, his intelligence quotient, his health limitations, his emotional stability, and even his volitional limits and behavioral patterns. Man is thus seen as inescapably determined by the genes which he inherits and from which he cannot escape.

The genetic factor cannot be denied, and its far-reaching significance is to be admitted. But that one is necessarily and wholly determined by genetics is to be challenged. Certainly it follows that genetic factors determine for many that they cannot in this bodily existence become an Einstein or a Hercules. Even if given the best of nutrition, the pigmy or midget cannot become a giant. No combination of zeal, effort, and surroundings can free the moron to become a genius. The holistic nature of man reflects the limits of body upon mind as well as the mind's power to control the body. Sexuality, whether male or female, is basically a genetic determination (although often psychologically redirected and sometimes surgically changed). The color of one's eyes is genetically determined. One born to white parents cannot be black, nor can one born to black parents be white. All this is obvious. But within these genetic factors, there is found a measure of freedom.

What one does with his genetic heritage and what one lets his genetic heritage do to him is not a matter of absolute determinism. One can accept or resist. He can modify an existence in ways which defy complete genetic determination. One need not think alone of a Helen Keller who could fight her way out of the darkness and isolation of a body born blind and deaf. She towers above most of us in her rejection of her genetic heritage. Less spectacular triumphs of the human spirit are to be found in every age and in every community. All concerns for the retarded and for their rehabilitation affirm the faith that all is not genetically determined.

Jesus grounded his whole mission on the promise of God that the captives could be freed, that the bludgeoned could be restored, that the blind might see, that the deaf might hear, that the lame might walk, that the lepers might be cleansed, that the dead might be raised, and that sinners might be forgiven and cleansed (Luke 4:18–19; 7:21 f.). The virgin birth of Jesus is not set forth to counter some doctrine of Adamic sin or to suggest the Gnostic doctrine that the flesh is evil, but to declare that "with God there is no impossibility" (Luke 1:37). God the Redeemer is not helpless before any genetic or social liability. He is on the side of salvation and hope, not on the side of frustration, defeat, and despair. He is the God who can raise the dead and set the sinner free, just as he could give a son to a maiden who had not known a husband (Luke 1:34).

More than Machine. Man is not "a machine into which we put what we call food and produce what we call thought," simply "an ingenious assembly of portable plumbing," for a machine is an invention of man, not the mystery of God's creation.[5] DeWolf correctly sees that it is a misunderstanding of man and encourages moral surrender and spiritual defeat to see man, as some do in the name of psychology, as an elaborate machine or a mass of dark emotional drives beyond consciousness and not subject to rational decision or control.[6] The psalmist points to the wonder of man which lifts him above the machine: "I am fearfully and wonderfully made!" (Ps. 139:14, KJV). Man is zoomorphic, but he is more; he is *anthrōpos.* He is more than machine and more than animal. Rust cogently argues that "the human personality and consciousness with its quality of self-transcendence is not to be reduced to a biochemical and physiological level."[7]

The relationship between mind and brain was discussed *in extenso* in Chapter 2. It was recognized that there is an interrelationship between the body chemistry and personal characteristics, an intimate bond between brain and mind; that in one's genetic heritage there are far-reaching implications for personal development.[8] But mind is more than a chain of physical cause and effect. Mind emerges within the structure of the physical order, but mind is more than brain. Mind cannot be reduced simply to matter or energy. The DNA molecules penetrate and help shape the human being physiologically and psychologically,[9] but this does not imply complete genetic determinism. That our personhood is bound up with the physiochemical forces of our bodies is congenial to the Hebrew view of man as holistic and psychosomatic, but not to the Greek view of man as a dichotomy of body and soul. But this holistic view of man does not imply ultimate genetic determinism, however much it implies conditioning and limits within which one has his personal existence.

Man is a moral being, sharing in the responsibility for the quality of his own existence. Moral accountability or responsibility is a meaningless anomaly without freedom.

There is a sense in which genes are the master of man: in a particular person the genes determine physical characteristics at least. But there is another sense in which man is the master of the genes. For centuries it has been known that "the chromosomes and genes present in all cells contain the hereditary information from the parents which determine the physical characteristics of their offspring," but now a new breakthrough has been made in solving the genetic code.[10] It may be that man now stands "on the threshold of being able to alter himself." [11] In 1952, Dr. James Watson and Dr. Francis Crick reported their findings on the structure of the DNA molecule (desoxyribonucleic acid). At some time in the future, "it may be possible to synthesize a complete DNA molecule that would contain the instructions necessary to build a complete human being according to a contrived plan," and it is even more probable that at least "certain portions of the DNA molecule can be modified to give desired characteristics." [12] Man, then, may be as able to determine genetic direction as genetics can determine man's direction.

The Disadvantaged. Apart from science's ability to control genetics, and in the face of the highly significant genetic factor, much freedom yet remains to man. It is true that some individuals seem to be so deprived genetically that there is little which they can do or which can be done for them. This follows especially where there is extreme incapacity in physical and mental endowment, although not all retardation is due to genetics. For most people there is much that they can do or which can be done for them in adjusting to what is given at birth or in compensating for any privation. We are responsible for what we do with what we have. Any recognition of moral value relating to man presupposes a measure of freedom and the rejection of absolute determinism, genetic or otherwise, else "moral" is reduced to no meaning at all. Moral implies choice and some freedom for choice.

There is no Biblical discussion of genetics as such. There is considerable concern in the Old Testament with the sufferings of children for the sins of the parents, a part only of which may be understood as biological transmission. Much of it concerns penalties relating to cultic practices and privileges (Ex. 20:5; 34:7; Num. 14:18; Deut. 5:9). Jesus abruptly brushed aside a question which presupposed the punishment of the child because of the parents' sins: "Lord, who sinned, this man or his parents, that he should be born blind?" (John 9:2). Jesus saw in the blind man's condition an opportunity to do good, but he rejected the theology which assumes inherited guilt and punishment. The blind man's future was not genetically determined. He received sight first at the physical level and then at the higher level of faith as he came to know "the light of the world" (John 9:5). Jesus came that those who see not may see and with the result that those unwilling to see lose their power to see (John 9: 39 f.).[13]

Social Bondage and Freedom

As with genetics, a case can be made for seeing both bondage and freedom in the context of environment and social conditioning. There are people who are socially disadvantaged and people who are socially advantaged. For millions of people, economic and cultural privations are so acute that they seem virtually trapped by them. Along with actual starvation there is yet more widespread malnutrition, which acutely limits one's power to function at any or all levels of existence. A starving child cannot keep pace in any area of life. Many who are considered lazy, shiftless, or inferior are simply hungry. They have never had nutrition at a subsistence or adequate level. Many live on land so poor and in an economic situation so adverse that there is virtually no way for them to surmount these conditions. What chance is there for a child born in a culvert in the subcontinent of Asia, with nothing around him but mud and other culverts filled with starving people?

Cultural Factors. Along with the economic privation which

can go far to determine a life are the cultural factors which can shape the attitudes of the little child and give him his values long before he has the maturity or options for freedom of choice. Fears, superstitions, prejudices, and their like can so blind, blight, and distort one's existence that he is denied any real freedom for fulfillment as a person. It is a part of the melancholy of life that the parents' sins are visited upon their children, not by biological or genetic transmission but by conditioning in the home and in the other structures of society, such as schools and even churches. Deliberately and inadvertently, consciously and unconsciously, parents induct their children into their own little worlds of darkness, phobias, prejudice, etc. Of course, there are positive factors of truth and beauty which also are communicated; but even so, the child is often more determined socially, for better or worse, by those in whose care his most formative years are spent than by his own choices. This dictates that enlightened Christian conscience must be actively concerned for favorable social change.

Social influence is one thing; absolute or inescapable determinism is another. Even in environmental and social conditions most threatening to personal freedom and fulfillment, there are possible escapes into authentic existence. Granted that the odds are against the ordinary person's transcending the conditions which tend to fix one's values and attitudes and to limit his options, there are before us constant reminders of something within an individual person which can resist, reject, and rebel against all that would reduce him to bondage. How else do we account for the emergence of so many free and authentic persons out of circumstances so hostile to what triumphs?

How do we account for Abraham Lincoln, who rose from the privation and provincialism of a log cabin on the Kentucky frontier to a stature lifted above the limits of time and place, belonging to the ages and to all nations and races, not simply to nineteenth-century America? How do we account for Clarence Jordan, founder of Koinonia Farm in Georgia, champion of such human rights as racial and economic justice, and of peace? Clarence Jordan was nurtured under the very environmental and social conditions which have produced certain racists, provincials, war hawks, and various expressions of bigotry. Something within an individual can resist, reject, and rebel against all that would determine for him his selfhood. Jesus himself in his radicality (radical means "root") is the supreme example of one who incarnated and proclaimed a kind of existence which at significant points was not dictated by, but instead was contrary to, that urged upon him by his home, his synagogue, and his historical situation (cf. Mark 3:31–35; Luke 4:16 ff.).

It is at just this point where something within one asserts itself against all that would determine him that true personal selfhood emerges. Life and liberty belong necessarily to personhood. True freedom includes freedom from automation, freedom to become oneself, "not the biological self of reflexes" or "of inexorable mechanisms that impede the flow of life." [14] A personage is the pseudo self created to reflect or please society. A person is an authentic self, living in the tension or polarities of freedom and bondage, constantly subjected to forces and factors which would shape one's existence and constantly asserting oneself in a freedom which defies all bondage.

The Satanic-Demonic. A special word is called for with respect to the "satanic" and/or "demonic" as it may relate to the individual or society. There is the disposition in theological circles to attribute much of the brutishness in human society to the "demonic." What is meant by this varies greatly. Some understand "demons" to have ontological objectivity, separate beings. Others employ the term for some dimension within individuals or society.

Wayne Oates, thinking primarily of "the destruction of personality," arrives at the balanced view which on the one hand respects the intuitive insights of the Biblical conceptions of demonism as intensely relevant to a proper understanding of the fragmentation of personality and on the other hand respects the findings of scientific study of mental illness.[15] He rejects the simplistic fallacy of equating the Biblical and scientific perspectives, i.e., reading a twentieth-century scientific understanding of mental illness back into the New Testament; and he finds equally misleading "the exclusivistic attitudes of both contemporary psycho-therapists on the one hand and the fundamentalistic religionists on the other," i.e., those who force a choice between either the Biblical or scientific view.[16] Some psychotherapists relegate to the dark ages the whole Biblical concern with demonism. On the other hand, some religionists understand "demons" in only a literal sense—in theory but not necessarily in their own practice. For when their own loved one requires it, they turn to medical specialists in the field of psychiatry rather than to an exorcist.[17]

Oates rejects Freud's view of man as a "still" picture with a fixed "anatomy of personality" in favor of the Biblical "moving picture of man in conflict with himself, of man as a wrestler with an inner law of his mind, crying for deliverance from his own destruction of himself," as man vainly worships gods that are "no gods," so elevating himself as to live "in distance" from God and neighbor, deifying a self-chosen part of his life as though it were the whole of life.[18]

Oates sees the demonic expressed in such destructive forces as fear. Seeing fear as not only the parent of hate but also the antithesis of love and deterrent to spiritual maturity, he points to I John 4:19–21, where "love is seen in all its perfection and maturity as the power which casts out, overcomes, and melts completely the demonic distortions of fear." [19] He also observes that "the 'casting out' or 'exorcistic' power of love is most vividly seen in the healing strength and the courageous love of Jesus in relation to the Gadarene demoniac." [20] This understanding of man's situation takes seriously forces and factors which assault man, but it makes no room for a demonic determinism which denies freedom to man.

The term "demonic" ("satanic" would be a better term here) does seem to be serviceable when one contemplates the uglier side of society's behavior, e.g., the slaughter of six million Jews under the Nazis or "carpet bombing" in Southeast Asia, and also the routine pressures by which society crushes the individual and denies him real personhood. But this can become an easy "passing of the buck" which fails to take account of the extent of man's

own freedom to choose his kind of existence. Man cannot "pass
the buck" of responsibility.

Probably the meaning of what is known Biblically as satanic
or demonic is the recognition that along with the prophetic insight that the root cause of man's condition is his own individual
sin is the other truth that behind many of the ills that men suffer
and inflict is their own collective responsibility.[21] Biblical writers,
in the New Testament far more so than in the Old Testament,
personified the hostile evil force encountered in the world, but
personification does not necessarily imply a real personality in
the term "Satan." [22] Illustration of this usage may be seen in
Matt. 6:24 and Luke 16:13 where "mammon" is spoken of as a
Lord (*kyrios*) but is actually hoarded wealth or gain. Biblical
writers tended to refer to all causation as personal rather than
impersonal, and it is sometimes unwise to differentiate too
sharply between the personal and impersonal.

They were *men* who thought up and exploited the Nazi myths
by which they justified genocide in Germany and the Soviet rape
of Hungary and Czechoslovakia. They were *men* who perpetrated
the atrocities of Dachau and My Lai. They are *men* who make
choices which lead to the bondage of fear, lust, greed, prejudice,
jealousy, and hate. It is man himself, created in the image of
God, who can take the roads which lead to bottomless pits of
ungodliness, inhumanity, and depravity. Man may thus be
caught up in the mob spirit, whether national, racial, or religious;
but it is individual man who yields to the mob by which he is
claimed and enslaved. In the final analysis, one must confess his
own sin, "I did it." Whatever may be said for the forces which
beat upon one from without, there is that which one *lets* be done
to himself as well as that which without his consent is done to
him. It is this former which is his guilt. "Demoniacs" are largely
victims of forces outside themselves and require the healing power
of love (Luke 8:26–39). Judas, into whom "Satan entered"
(John 13:27), required nothing short of repentance (Heb.
12:17).

Jesus addressed men as capable of infinite good and of infinite evil. He could challenge men to the kind of existence in which one is "pure in heart" (Matt. 5:8), suffers all manner of evil for righteousness' sake (Matt. 5:10 f.), avoids even the lustful look (Matt. 5:27–30), turns the cheek to the offender (Matt. 5:39), goes the second mile in service to the undeserving (Matt. 5:41), loves both neighbor and enemy (Matt. 5:43 f.), and accepts perfection as his goal (Matt. 5:48). Jesus also addressed man as one in need of daily forgiveness (Matt. 6:12) and as capable of inflicting such evil upon people as innocent little children that even death is to be preferred to such existence (Matt. 18:6). To this extent Jesus recognized the freedom of man and the bondage of man. He addressed man as free to trust God, to trust love, to trust truth, and to open himself to all which leads to authentic, personal existence. He also saw man as free to choose bondage, free to give himself to all that is false, phony, ugly, enslaving, and otherwise dehumanizing. Never did Jesus address man as so determined by genetics or society that he was without freedom or responsibility. Man may become "satanic," but the "satanic" is something belonging to man himself.

According to Mark 1:24, the demons cried out, "You have come to destroy us." In a real sense Jesus did destroy the demons. When Jesus came, many lived in daily fear of demons, the fear that they determined one's fate, that a demon could be drunk from a cup of water, that demons lurked in trees or rocks, etc. To people today who can go a single day without even thinking of demons, the demons have been destroyed, at least in the sense known and feared in the ancient world. Jesus "destroyed" the demons not only through bringing the power of the kingdom of God, but by radically shifting the base for an understanding of evil. He pointed to the human heart as the source of the impurity which is released in the world (Mark 7:14–23). Käsemann puts it in focus: "Jesus destroys the basis of classical demonology which rests on the conception that man is threatened by the powers of the universe and thus at bottom fails to recognize the threat which is offered to the universe by man himself." [23] Jesus "knew the evil of the human heart and its demonic power and took possession of this heart for God." [24]

ELECTION AND FREEDOM

If man is wholly determined neither by genetics nor by environmental and social impingements, does it follow that he is determined by God's will? Some would have it so. The Stoics believed in a divine determinism or predestination. This was also a tenet among the Pharisees at the beginning of the Christian era. In the Christian community this has been a widely held view, especially among those in the tradition of John Calvin. Some see predestination as the inescapable corollary to God's sovereignty. If God be absolutely sovereign, how can any decision be made except by his will? Carried to its logical conclusion, reasoning on this premise would have it that everything man is and does is by divine will. This would not only mean the loss of human freedom but the reduction of man to a mere thing. Moreover, it would have frightening implications for God himself. Sovereignty would become tyranny and man's "freedom" a myth. If all that occurs—wars, genocide, rape, exploitation, slavery—be by divine determination, then existence is evil to its very foundations.

To explain evil and misfortune by a distinction between God's active will and God's permissive will, as is done by some theologians, is to fill the room with more smoke than light. God's will is in no sense behind evil. God's will is behind the freedom which makes possible both good and evil, but God's will is not behind the evil which is misused freedom. It follows that God permits evil because he permits freedom, but it unduly confuses the issue to join "permissive will" to evil. It is important to "distinguish the things which differ" (Rom. 2:18; Phil. 1:10). God wills freedom; he wills good; he does not will evil (cf. Rom. 12:2; II Peter 3:9).

The doctrine of divine election is primary in the Scriptures of ancient Judaism and of Christianity. But election does not mean determination nor predestination. Election is God's initiative in his relationship with man, in creation, revelation, and redemption. Election is not coercion. It is not the imposition of God's will upon man's. There is no necessary conflict between God's election of man and man's freedom of response. Election does not mean that God predestines some for salvation and some for damnation. Election means that God does not wait for man but rather that he takes the initiative in moving toward man (John 15:16).

The whole Biblical perspective is that of God's movement toward man. In this is a striking contrast with most religions outside the Judeo-Christian tradition. In most of the world's religions man is seen as having to bear the burden of initiative in his relationship with God. Man has to seek and find God. Man has to appease his god or gods. Man has to earn acceptance or reward or at least exemption from divine punishment. Man's efforts may take the shape of ritual offerings, moral behavior, or creedal acceptability. In any case, man has to bridge the gap between himself and his god. Not so in Judaism and in Christianity. There God is seen not only as creator but also as revealer and redeemer. God has made man to seek after God (Acts 17:26 f.), but God is already active in making himself knowable to man (Rom. 1:19 f.). God is one who comes to his people to save them (Isa. 40:3; Matt. 3:3).

Calling. Closely related to the concept of election is that of calling. In Matt. 22:14 the terms are distinguished: "Many are called (*klētoi*) but few are elected (*eklektoi*)." In the parable of the marriage feast, many are invited (the meaning of "called"), but only a few are accepted (the *eklektoi* are ones selected or approved). It is explicit here that "calling" or "invitation" is not coercive. The king's "calling" or "invitation" opened up for the potential guests the possibility of participating in the king's banquet. Only at the king's initiative did this become a possibility. They could not come uninvited. They could not "crash the party." But the invitation was not coercive. It left an option for the invited guests. They could choose not to come. Of course, their choice carried with it implications for joyous participation or woeful self-exclusion. Both the king's sovereignty over his banquet and the invited persons' freedom of response remained in effect.

Paul made much of "calling" (*klēsis*) and its cognates. He did not make Matthew's distinction between "calling" and "election" (cf. Rom. 8:30, 33), for he reserved the term "called" for those who make positive response to God's calling. In using the term, Paul looks back upon salvation and thus accounts for its origin. Salvation is always God's work, from beginning to end. By tracing salvation to "calling" or "election," Paul denies to man any boast in himself and requires that if man boasts at all it be in God's saving grace (Rom. 3:19; I Cor. 1:31).

Paul saw all the saints (the saved) as called (*klētoi*). Even the problem-ridden church at Corinth was made up of "called saints" (I Cor. 1:2). They were saints by calling. "Called" translates an adjective; it is not a part of the verb. The basic calling is the calling to Christ, the calling to discipleship. There are further callings, as to apostleship. Paul identified himself as a "called apostle" (I Cor. 1:1). Again, *klētos* is an adjective, not a part of the verb. Both the basic call to discipleship and further callings into particular roles of ministry, like apostleship, are at God's initiative, not man's.

Although the call to apostleship is exclusive, limited to some only, there is no indication that the call to discipleship excludes anyone. Although Paul applies the term "called" only to the saved, he does not imply that the lost are lost because they were not called. He never refers to the "uncalled" or to those not called. The opposite to "the called" are those who are disobedient. The opposite of election is not predestination to perdition but self-incurred unbelief.[25] Those under "the wrath of God" (Rom. 1:18) are not those from whom God has withheld himself, but those who have "refused to have God in their knowledge" (Rom. 1:28) even though God had made himself knowable to them (Rom. 1:19 f.). Speaking primarily of Gentiles who rejected God's overtures, Paul says that God "delivered them over" (Rom. 1:24, 26, 28), the context indicating that he meant that God delivers stubborn men over to their own choices. God allows men to self-destruct, if they insist upon it. He offers himself to men but does not coerce acceptance.

Speaking primarily of Israel, Paul comes to the same conclusion. If Jews are lost, they are lost for precisely the reason

Gentiles are lost, not because of any divine determination or failing but because the offered salvation is rejected. In a carefully constructed passage, Paul shows that God's salvation is as near as the word in one's mouth, as near as faith in one's heart (Rom. 10:7–13). All man needs to do is trust and call upon the God who already has entrusted himself to man and called out to man. God has drawn near to man, for God's Christ is not in some inaccessible heaven or in the abyss with the dead; he is as near as the preached word (Rom. 10:8). The word has been preached; it is accessible and it is intelligible (Rom. 10:14–20). One problem alone is beyond divine determination, man's own unpredictable will. Man can hear or turn a deaf ear. He can trust or distrust. If man remains lost, it is by man's choice and not God's determination. In the face of man's refusal to respond, God can only say, "All the day long I stretched out my hands to a people disobedient and gainsaying" (Rom. 10:21).

Election and calling are Biblical terms and express a concept basic to Old and New Testaments. It is God who opens up the possibilities for man's salvation. But never does this become a fate imposed upon man. Were that the case, there would be no salvation at all. To determine that some be "saved" and some "lost" would in fact be to determine that all be lost. "Salvation" by determination would be damnation raised to the nth degree, for man without freedom is no man at all. Man manipulated is man destroyed. But this distorted idea of "salvation" belongs to Biblical "interpretation" and not to Biblical affirmation. The Bible is primarily the story of God's action in saving man. God's way of salvation is the hard way, that of persuasion, not of compulsion. Broken things can be fixed but broken humanity must be healed. Fixing is something done to a passive object. Healing is something done in and through a responsive subject. Salvation is not God's overcoming our humanity but his gracious work of restoring our humanity—in a relationship in which paradoxically we find our freedom by yielding it to God's sovereign claim upon us.

The Wrath of God. This awesome phrase may seem to teach that man after all may be victim of divine determination. The term "wrath" (*orgē*) is found numerous times in the New Testament, especially in writings attributed to Paul. Sometimes *orgē* seems to denote the emotion of anger (Mark 3:5; Eph. 4:31; Col. 3:8; I Tim. 2:8; Heb. 3:11; 4:3; James 1:19 f.). More often it seems to point not to an emotion but to judgment upon sin and the results of sin. The "day of wrath" (Rom. 2:5) and the "coming wrath" (Matt. 3:7; Luke 3:7; I Thess. 1:10) refer to judgment, when the consequences of one's sins overtake him.

The full phrase "the wrath of God" appears only in John 3:36 and Rev. 19:15, but the anarthrous *orgē Theou* (God's wrath) in Rom. 1:18 probably has the same force. In Rev. 6:16 there is reference to "the wrath of the Lamb." The simple phrase "the wrath" is more frequent. Significantly, it is in Rom. 1:18–32 alone that "God's wrath" is the explicit subject of a New Testament writer (see our discussion in Chapter 1). Only in Rom. 1:18–32 is the concept analyzed *in extenso*. But in this passage Paul does "spell out" precisely and in great detail what he means by "God's wrath," its nature, cause, and consequences. Here if anywhere in the New Testament one may gain an understanding of "wrath," at least in the thought of Paul.

It is significant that Rom. 1:18–32 is completely void of apocalyptic imagery. There is no analogy to "fire and brimstone." There is no suggestion of punishment imposed arbitrarily or externally. There is something more terrifying. There is the picture of man's awesome power to reject God's overture and to self-destruct. Man can choose not to have God in his knowledge (Rom. 1:28). Man can choose a course in which he elevates the creature to the position of the Creator (Rom. 1:25). It is the frightening picture of what man can do to himself. He can trade off the potential of knowledge and vision for foolishness and darkness (Rom. 1:21 f.). Man can choose the way which results in the breakdown of his moral and ethical structure (Rom. 1:24–27) and the breakup of the human family (Rom. 1:28–32). This is not a fate imposed upon man. This does not represent a divine predestination or even the "permissive will" of God. This in no sense represents the will of God. It represents man's rejection of God's good will.

Three times (Rom. 1:24, 26, 28) Paul affirms with respect to rebellious men that "God gave them over . . ." To whom? To what? The context implies that God gave man over to man himself. God honors the freedom given man in creation. God does not override man's freedom, even if man abuses this freedom to his own ruin. God warns, pleads, and offers himself; but God does not cross over the line which distinguishes persuasion from coercion. God gives man over to himself, even if man plunges ahead into darkness and depravity. With the freedom of choice are the consequences: self-exclusion from God, moral-ethical breakdown (even to the reduction of existence to perverted sex) [26] and social breakup (with all its ugly antisocial attitudes). This is God's "wrath." It is his will to make us free, at the calculated risk of ruin.

Predestination. The idea of determination comes to expression, if anywhere in the New Testament, in the words *horizein* and *proorizein*. The RSV renders *horizein* variously: "determined" (Luke 22:22; Acts 11:29; 17:26), "ordained" (Acts 10:42), "appointed" (Acts 17:31). Not one of these English words is to be pressed, for each is somewhat arbitrary. The idea of determination is not certainly present in any of these examples, and it is clearly absent in Rom. 1:4, where the idea is that of disclosure: "designated Son of God in power." In Heb. 4:7 the original (etymological) force of *horizein* is best preserved: "he . . . defineth a certain day" (ASV). *Horizein* is "to mark out," "to define." From this Greek word is derived the English "horizon." The Greek *horos* is the word for boundary. In its various contexts in the New Testament, *horizein* is not far from this original idea of "designation" or "marking out." The further idea of determination may be implied but not clearly so. Even the English "determine" is ambiguous, for it may imply "fixing the boundaries" or "discovering the boundaries."

The idea of determination is more likely in *proorizein*. This is especially indicated in Acts 4:28, "Whatever thy hand and thy plan (*boulē*) had predestined to take place." The case for absolute determination is weakened by the fact that "both Herod and Pontius Pilate with the Gentiles and the peoples of Israel" (Acts

4:27) are charged with rage, vanity, and rebellion (Acts 4:25 f.). Surely the will of God is not behind rage, vanity, and rebellion, else God is immoral (unthinkable!) and man is nonmoral, merely a puppet manipulated by God. The book of Acts does not exonerate those who crucified Jesus, and this must enter into one's understanding of the sense in which God "predestined" the crucifixion of Jesus. Probably the best understanding of the saying is that, in retrospect, the disciples saw God as anticipating what occurred and as retaining his sovereignty (Acts 4:24) and initiative in the whole event. The intention was to stress God's sovereignty, not to make God responsible for men's murderous acts.

This careful distinction between God's part and man's part is clearly drawn in Acts 2:23: "this Jesus, delivered up according to the definite plan (*hōrismenēi boulēi*) and foreknowledge of God—you crucified and killed by the hands of lawless men." God's will is behind the giving up, not behind the killing. The will of lawless men alone is behind the killing. Elsewhere the crucifixion of Jesus is called rejection (Mark 12:10; John 1:11), betrayal (Mark 8:31; 14:41), and murder (Acts 7:52; I Thess. 2:14 f.).[27] These heavy charges are incompatible with the concept of determination. Paradoxically, Jesus had to die (i.e., to reject the disposition to cling to his own life), but men did not have to "reject," "betray," and "murder" him. God's will was behind what Jesus did. Man's will, not God's, was behind what wicked men did to him.

The idea of predestination seems to appear in Rom. 8:29, "For those whom he foreknew he also predestined (*proōrisen*) to be conformed to the image of his Son." The original force of *proorizein* suits the passage, meaning that God designed or marked it out ("horizoned") that we be like his Son. So understood, the emphasis is upon the goal which God had from the beginning in his redemptive work. The whole chapter is concerned to give assurance that for those "in Christ Jesus" (Rom. 8:1) there is now "no condemnation" (Rom. 8:1) and no separation from God (Rom. 8:35–39). God completes what he begins. He knows where he is going before he begins. Salvation is no accident, either in its inception or its consummation (cf. Eph. 1:5, 11).

Paul's idea is not that God selects some for salvation and determines its accomplishment out of his will alone. Much in Romans becomes meaningless or contradictory on this assumption. Paul's anguish and agony over his fellow Jews is meaningless on the theory of divine determination of everything (cf. Rom. 9:1–3; 10:1, 21). The same *proorizein* is used for the "wisdom of God," which God "decreed (*proōrisen*) before the ages for our glorification" (I Cor. 2:7). The wisdom which was "hidden" was also a wisdom "marked out" or "designated" for our glory. The idea of "determination" or "predestination" is not well suited to the idea of God's wisdom. God's wisdom was a fact, not a purposed accomplishment. It was a wisdom to be disclosed, not to be determined.

"Predestination," then, does not imply that God determines man's fate and the occurrences of his life. It expresses faith's recognition of the initiative of God in man's salvation. It is the recognition that God has a plan from the beginning and that he follows through in his designs (Rom. 8:28–30). When salvation is accomplished, it is because of God's studied purpose, not through man's initiative, virtue, or works. To go the further step in the conclusion that God arbitrarily determines fate and fortune is unwarranted and reduces all to nonsense.

Chapter 6

SAINTS
YET SINNERS

Luther was on target when he described the Christian as *simul justus et peccator* (at the same time just and sinner). We are, indeed, "saints yet sinners." The truest faith confesses, "I believe, help thou mine unbelief" (Mark 9:24). One who boasts that he never has doubts is fooling only himself. Likewise, God's "saints" are to pray daily, "Forgive us our sins" (Luke 11:4). By every test, a person under redemption is a mixture of faith and doubt, commitment and reservation, love and hate, loyalty and disloyalty, hope and despair.

It has been said that the "Old Testament has no heroes or saints." [1] This is subject to challenge. There are both heroes and villains, saints and sinners, in both the Old and the New Testament. Moreover, in one and the same person may be found hero and villain, saint and sinner. There is much truth in Barth's striking claim: "Jacob is always Esau also, and in the eternal 'moment' of revelation Esau is also Jacob." [2] It is a part of the integrity of the Bible that it dares to paint men as they are, "warts and all." One may think of Abraham, Jacob, Moses, Jonah, John the Baptist, John, Peter, and Paul. Each is highly esteemed, and yet each is portrayed in both strength and weakness.

Abraham is the father of the faithful and a model in faith, yet Scripture does not conceal the fact that he sometimes doubted, showed fear, sometimes lied, sometimes acted out of shortsighted selfishness. Fearing that he might be killed (Gen. 20:11), he once lied, saying that Sarah was his sister instead of his wife, willing thus to sacrifice her honor for his own physical safety. Jacob became Israel, "Prince of God," and he embodied many great traits of character; but he could also be tricky, deceitful, greedy, selfish, willing to deceive his father, cheat his brother, and outwit his father-in-law (cf. Gen. 27:1–38; 30:37–43). Moses could lose his temper, and he could seek credit for power that was not his own (cf. Ex. 2:11–14; Num. 20:11 f.). David is called a man after God's own heart (I Sam. 13:14; Acts 13:22), and he stands as high in the New Testament as in the Old, yet David's grievous sins of adultery, murder, and deceit are painfully exposed (II Sam. 11:2 to 12:15). Jonah was a great prophet (cf. Matt. 12:41), yet Jonah could be so provincial, selfish, and mean that he could actually desire the destruction of a great city filled with men, women, and children (Jonah 4:1–5, 10 f.).

In the New Testament as in the Old, the sins of the saints are exposed along with their virtues. John the Baptist was "more than a prophet" and among the highest of those "born of women" (Matt. 11:9, 11), yet he was seemingly uncertain about the basic character of the Messianic function (Matt. 11:2–6). John the Baptist thought so much in terms of "the axe" and the winnowing "fan" that he needed to see that in the work of the Messiah which is symbolized in the "dove" (Matt. 3:10, 12, 16). John, who became the apostle of love, at one point tried to hinder the good work of another (Luke 9:49); with his brother James, he once proposed destruction by fire for a Samaritan village that had refused hospitality to Jesus and his disciples (Luke 9:54). On another occasion James and John immodestly and naïvely asked for the positions of chief honor in the anticipated kingdom of Christ (Mark 10:35–37). Peter was in many respects the "prince of the apostles," yet he could become so frightened as to lie three times, denying that he even knew Jesus—this at the time of Jesus' greatest need for support (Mark 14:66–72). Peter could also betray the vision that with God there is no partiality among men (Acts 10:15, 34), for at Antioch, intimidated by new arrivals from Jerusalem, he withdrew from the table fellowship which included Gentile and Jewish believers (Gal. 2:11–21). There is evidence that James (presumably the half brother to Jesus) actually opposed such "mixed" fellowship, while Peter personally accepted it but lacked the courage to stand up for it in the presence of certain ones "who came from James" (Gal. 2:12).

Although Christians readily accept the explicit New Testament evidence that Peter was a mixture of strength and weakness, of devotion and fear, there is not generally the same disposition to recognize the faults of Paul. True, there are those who have little patience with Paul and write him off as hopeless. It seems to be easier to be blind either to Paul's faults or to his virtues than to see them in their true proportion. Paul was a man of conflict,[3] with great strength and serious limitations. Late in life he confessed that he had not yet attained the goal toward which Christ had pointed him (Phil. 3:12–14). His many conflicts with other people were not due entirely to the faults of others. For example, when he and Barnabas had sharp words over John Mark and broke up their missionary team, it does not necessarily follow that Paul was less wrong than Barnabas (Acts 15:36–41). Paul was honest and humble enough to confess that his "treasure" and ours is entrusted to "earthen vessels" (II Cor. 4:7). Paul was an "earthen vessel," and his "earthen" nature is as obvious as the fact of the "treasure" contained in this authentic servant of Christ. He personally had to struggle to keep faith with the vision which guided his life as a disciple of Christ. One of his deepest insights was that "there can be neither Jew nor Greek, there can be neither bond nor free, there can be no male and female, for we are one in Christ Jesus" (Gal. 3:28; cf. Rom. 10:12; I Cor. 12:13; Col. 3:11). The distinctions of nationality, legal status, and sex have their significance but not "in Christ." Paul followed through in the application of this vision to Jew and Gentile, refusing to make one secondary to the other. In salvation, in table fellowship, and in privilege, Jew and Gentile were equal. But when it came to the status and privilege of women, Paul still preferred to keep them relatively quiet in church and to require them to wear veils as a sign of their subordination to men (cf. I Cor. 11:2–16; 14:33–36). At this point there is tension between

Paul's vision and Paul's practice. Paul himself distinguished between the words of Jesus and his own opinion, and he did not claim final authority for his own opinions (I Cor. 7:10, 12).

The New Testament claims perfection for Jesus alone, not for any apostle or other follower. The apostles and the other followers were saints, yet sinners. Our fallibility dogs us every step of the way, even as we fight evil in ourselves or in others. Barth is right in saying: "All reformers are Pharisees. . . . Deprive a Total Abstainer, a really religious Socialist, a Churchman, or a Pacifist, of the PATHOS of moral indignation, and you have broken his backbone." [4] We soil everything we touch, even in our crusades for good. We remain sinner-saints.

SAINTS BY CALLING

Christians in Corinth (I Cor. 1:2) and Rome (Rom. 1:7) are addressed as "called saints" (*klētois hagiois*). Christians often are referred to simply as "saints" (cf. II Cor. 1:1; Eph. 1:1; Phil. 1:1; Col. 1:2; I Thess. 3:13; II Thess. 1:10; I Tim. 5:10; Philemon, v. 5; Heb. 6:10; Jude, v. 3; and Rev. 5:8). As observed in Chapter 5, "called" is an adjective, not a part of the verb. Saints are such by divine calling. The initiative is with God in salvation as well as in creation and revelation. The status of saints is a possibility brought about by God's initiative. Saints are persons who have responded to God's call.

"Called saints" does not mean simply "named" saints. Neither is the Greek phrase properly rendered "called to be saints" (KJV). This may falsely imply that sainthood is yet future, whereas in fact those then and there, whether in Corinth or Rome, were addressed as saints. Sainthood is not some second or later stage which takes place after the initial stage of justification. Sainthood belongs to salvation at its inception, from the very first. There is no such thing as being saved without being sanctified. One is a "saint" just as soon as he is "saved." There are no "unsanctified" Christians. There are no Christians who are not saints, yet sinners.

Sainthood is not the privileged status of a limited number of Christians. Two fallacies find no support in the New Testament: (1) the idea that of the "saved" only those who are sinless or near sinless are "sanctified" and (2) the idea that the saints are found only among the dead who have been elevated to such status. The New Testament recognizes "saints" among the living, and the term is as inclusive as are "those being saved." I Corinthians should be decisive for these facts. The letter is addressed to "the church in Corinth" and these are "called saints" (I Cor. 1:2). These are the ones "being saved" as contrasted with those "being destroyed" (I Cor. 1:18). The church at Corinth was plagued with problems of division, incest, litigation, disorders in worship services, pride, etc. These people, nonetheless, were addressed as "saints." To Paul the saints were neither the blessed dead alone nor sinless or near sinless persons. They were the "garden variety" of everyday Christians.

Set Apart. The original idea in sanctification or holiness[5] was that of separation. To sanctify was to set apart for a certain purpose. What was set apart was "holy" or "sanctified." Places, vessels, seasons, or persons could be set apart, sanctified, or considered holy. Among pagans, even prostitutes who comprised a part of the cultic practices (fertility cults, etc.) were termed "holy women" or "saints." They were set apart or sanctified to religious prostitution. In Judaism and early Christianity, land could be holy (Matt. 4:5; 24:15; II Peter 1:18), utensils in cultic usage were holy (Matt. 23:17, 19), seasons (Ex. 16:23; 20:8) and people (I Peter 3:5) were holy.

In ancient Greek, *hagios* ("holy") signified the object of awe in either the sense of reverence or a curse, depending upon the perspective. What to one was revered was by another feared or despised. The cognate *hagēs* approximated the sense of *katharos,* with the sense of "cleansed" or "pure." In the Septuagint, *hagios* translates the Hebrew *kadhosh,* the root meaning of which is "to separate," in contrast to the profane.[6] *Hagios* and its cognates were originally cultic, with no necessary moral connotation. The wide range of English words such as "sanctify," "sacred," "consecrated," and "holy" all translate the same Greek cognates and are not to be pressed for distinction.

Moral and ethical connotations did not originally belong to the idea of holiness or sanctity. This follows from the fact that the idea of holiness belonged as normally to things as to persons. It follows also from the fact that it could designate persons who, at least from Biblical perspective, were engaged in immoral practices, as the "holy women" engaged in sacred prostitution. In the Old Testament and the New the further idea of moral-ethical meaning comes in, but the older idea of simple setting apart remains. Even Jesus "sanctifies himself" in behalf of his people (cf. John 17:19), where there is no hint that he undergoes moral cleansing. He simply devotes himself to the good of his people. Christians are people set apart by divine initiative and to divine purpose.

Moral-Ethical Renewal. Biblical usage includes the original idea of "setting apart," found also in pagan religious usage; but it goes far beyond this. It has special concern for the moral and ethical implications of holiness or sanctification. This results from the fact that it is God who sanctifies, and he sanctifies persons to himself. To be holy as he is holy (Lev. 11:44; I Peter 1:16) is not just to be "set apart" but to acquire moral qualities which derive from God.

That "sanctified" may be used in the New Testament with strong moral implications is inescapable in I Cor. 6:11: "But ye were washed, but ye were sanctified, but ye were justified." Those so described are set over against "fornicators," "idolaters," "adulterers," "catamites," "homosexuals," "thieves," "greedy people," "drunkards," "slanderers," and "robbers" (I Cor. 6:9 f.). There are no cultic ideas here. Those ruled out of the kingdom of God (I Cor. 6:10) are morally and ethically bankrupt. Those who already have been sanctified are morally and ethically unlike these people.

Sanctification is clearly moral when contrasted with fornication. "This is God's will, your sanctification, that you abstain from fornication" (I Thess. 4:3). The context is conclusive for actual purity, not cultic purity. The idea of "setting apart" is not the full one here. Paul's statement is to be understood at face value, in its simplest meaning. The same moral demand is present in I Thess. 4:4 and 7, where English translations usually employ the word "holiness." The identical Greek word, *hagiasmos,* is behind the translations "sanctification" (I Thess. 4:3) and "holiness" (I Thess. 4:4, 7). Holiness is linked to "honor" (I Thess. 4:4) and contrasted with "uncleanness" (I Thess. 4:7), which contextually means "fornication" (I Thess. 4:3).

Sanctification is linked with righteousness in Rom. 6:19, 22 (cf. also I Cor. 1:30). Those who once gave themselves to "impurity" and to "greater and greater iniquity" are now challenged to give themselves to "the righteousness" which results in "sanctification" (Rom. 6:19). That it is real righteousness and not forensic is seen in Rom. 6:20, where it is contrasted with "sin." Freed from sin and "enslaved" to God, the Romans now have their "fruit" in terms of the sanctification whose "end" is eternal life (Rom. 6:22).

In I Tim. 2:15 "sanctification" probably means "purity" as it applies to the writer's understanding of the proper role for women. In II Tim. 2:21 one is "sanctified" or "consecrated" (RSV) if he "purifies himself," i.e., "departs from iniquity" (II Tim. 2:19). In Rev. 22:11 the moral nature of sanctification is implied in the judgment: "Let the evildoer still do evil, and the filthy still be filthy, and the righteous still do right, and the holy still be holy."

The prayer in I Thess. 5:23 is for a sanctification understood as wholeness: "May the God of peace himself sanctify you wholly (*holoteleis*); and may your spirit and soul and body be kept sound (*holoklēron*) and blameless at the coming of our Lord Jesus Christ." In every way the verse stresses wholeness, completion, soundness, balance. The phrase "spirit and soul and body" may reflect a trichotomous perspective, but probably it is simply popular language for emphasis upon the total self. The adjectives *holotelēs* and *holoklēros* stress thoroughness and balance respectively, and each stresses soundness. Even the phrase "the God of peace" points to God's work in sanctification as that of making one whole or complete. The Greek *eirēnē* preserves the Old Testament concept of *shalom,* peace as well-being or wholeness. The idea is not cultic or forensic. It is that of personal health and fulfillment.

Goodness in Men. From Biblical perspective may one speak of a good man? Some would say not. Karl Barth, at least in his early and desperately needed revolt against the liberal theology which found nothing essentially wrong with man, overreacted. He went too far in seeing the image of God as completely destroyed in man.[7] But Scripture does recognize goodness in man. Alongside the recognition that salvation is God's work from beginning to end and in no sense man's achievement stands the view that there is goodness in man. It is there as the result of God's own goodness and his good work.

It is true that in the absolute sense only God is good. Jesus declared: "No one is good but God alone" (Mark 10:18; cf. Matt. 19:17; Luke 18:19). Only God is always good and wholly good. On the other hand man is never fully good, and there is always some mixture of evil in his good, such as being "proud of his humility." Paul's confession applies to us all: "For I know that there does not dwell in me, that is, in my flesh, anything good" (Rom. 7:18). By "flesh" Paul does not here mean the physical flesh. He refers to himself apart from God, man trying to go it alone. Of himself, apart from God, man has no goodness in him. But man may be more than "flesh." Man related to God may become good, or be made good. To make man good is God's own good work in salvation.

In the Lukan writings two men are mentioned by name and called good. Joseph of Arimathea, a member of the Jewish council, is said to be "a good (*agathos*) and righteous (*dikaios*) man" (Luke 23:50). Barnabas is said to be "a good man and full of the Holy Spirit and faith" (Acts 11:24). There is no reason to reject the plain meaning of these words. It is not implied that these men were perfect or sinless, but they are seen as good men. It is not implied that they achieved goodness apart from God, but there was goodness in these men.

Jesus himself addressed men as capable of both good and evil.

That he saw men as sinners in need of forgiveness and cleansing is abundantly clear. He saw that men need daily to pray for forgiveness and to forgive others (cf. Matt. 6:12). Jesus saw that men were evil even at their best, as when giving good gifts to their children (Matt. 7:11). But he also saw goodness in man and saw man as capable of great goodness. He recognized that there were "the evil and the good" among the men to whom God gave sunshine and rain (Matt. 5:45). He described "the good man" as bringing forth good out of his good treasure (Matt. 12:35; Luke 6:45). He described the Messianic banquet as bringing together bad men and good men (Matt. 22:10), and at the judgment he saw the sorting out of the "good and faithful servant" (Matt. 25:21) and the "wicked and slothful servant" (Matt. 25:26). He also saw men as capable of becoming "the salt of the earth" and "the light of the world" (Matt. 5:13 f.). He saw men as loving their enemies (Matt. 5:44), turning the cheek when struck (Matt. 5:39), and going the second mile, even for a Roman oppressor (Matt. 5:41). He even called men to perfection, man's true goal, however short he may fall of it (Matt. 5:48).

Even Paul, the great proponent of salvation by God's grace alone, recognized goodness in man. Distinctions are probably not to be pressed between "a righteous man" (*dikaios*) and "a good man" (*agathos*) in Rom. 5:7, but at least Paul is thinking of actual goodness, for these are contrasted with "sinners" (Rom. 5:8). He could hardly have been more emphatic than in the concluding parts of Romans: "I am confident, my brothers, even I myself, concerning you, that you yourselves are full of goodness (*agathōsunēs*) . . ." (Rom. 15:14). Even in Galatians, where he is so concerned to deny that salvation is a human achievement, Paul entreats us to "do good to all men" (Gal. 6:10). The Thessalonians are admonished always "to do good to one another and to all" (I Thess. 5:15). The Colossians are to bear fruit "in every good work" (Col. 1:10). In Ephesians—whether written by Paul or a Pauline follower—we are seen as "created in Christ Jesus for good works" (Eph. 2:10), and man can do good

(Eph. 6:8). Women are to find their true beauty in "good deeds" (I Tim. 2:10). The man of God is to be "equipped for every good work" (II Tim. 2:21; 3:17).

Goodness belongs to the fruit of the Spirit (Gal. 5:22). It is not man's own achievement, for basically it is God's work in man. Again, it is not God's achievement apart from man. It is God's good work achieved in those responsive to God's gracious work (I Cor. 15:10). This goodness is not forensic or "imputed." It is authentic goodness wrought into the existence of man as God's own glorious achievement. It is true, as Ernst Käsemann likes to say, that Jesus did not come to make pious people more pious. But Jesus did most certainly come to make bad people good! He came to give not only a new standing, acceptance, but also new life, a new kind of existence. The saints are not sinless but they are people whom God is making good. The ethical question is not a bourgeois conceit, nor is the goal of goodness in man a heresy.

Real Righteousness. It is regrettable that the term "justification" understood as "counting right those who are not right" has come to represent New Testament thought to so many. There is a most significant teaching in the New Testament developed around various cognate words built upon the Greek root *dik-*;[8] but as commonly employed in theology, "justification" does not do justice to that teaching. The crux of the matter is that in salvation God brings about real righteousness in man, not mere forensic righteousness. God does accept sinners, but he does not accept sin, just as a physician accepts sick people but does not make peace with sickness. The whole point is to bring about cure, not to count well one who is not well or to count righteous one who is not righteous.

Käsemann rejects as false the alternative offered by "the long and bitter dispute about whether the apostle [Paul] preached a forensic-imputative or an effective righteousness," holding that this is simply directed against two opposing modern misinterpretations.[9] He rejects the view that Paul proclaimed an "as if" kind of righteousness which has no earthly equivalent and also rejects the view of righteousness as "a gift which could be detached from the giver and transferred to our possession." [10] This is a welcomed statement, especially in view of such continuing talk as Conzelmann's as he speaks of "appropriated righteousness" (*die übereignete Gerechtigkeit* is literally "transferred righteousness").[11] Although Käsemann seems to reject the concept of "effective righteousness" as well as that of "forensic-imputative," he comes close to the former as he speaks of the "creative power" of God's word in Paul, as well as in the Old Testament and Judaism.[12] Whatever terms may best express it, at least for Paul and for the New Testament as a whole the concern is for real righteousness and not for "as if" or imputed righteousness, and the thought of transferring righteousness from one to another, like exchanging a gift, is absurd.

It may come as a real surprise to some to learn that the Greek word *dikaiōsis,* usually translated "justification," appears only twice in the New Testament (Rom. 4:25; 5:18). In Rom. 4:25 it is set over against "transgressions" (*paraptōmata*), and probably Paul means to say that Christ was "delivered over on account of our transgressions and raised with a view to our being made righteous." The English "justification" hardly suits here. In Rom. 5:18, *dikaiōsin* is set over against *katakrima* ("condemnation") and in this context possibly refers to the "acquittal that brings life." [13] It could also denote a putting into the right way.

The verb form *dikaioun,* commonly translated "to justify," connotes far more than "to count right." Depending upon context, it may mean to vindicate or find right, or it may mean to make free or pure. In the Gospels it invariably means to vindicate or find one out as right. Wisdom is "justified" by her fruits, i.e., vindicated, found true or right (Matt. 11:19; Luke 7:35). Out of one's words one is "justified" or "condemned," i.e., found right or found wrong (Matt. 12:37). When the people and the taxgatherers "justified God" they did not "count him right even though he was not right." They found him to be right (Luke 7:29). The lawyer tried to vindicate himself, prove himself right (Luke 10:29), as did the Pharisees on another occasion (Luke 16:15). When they prayed in the Temple, the humble taxgatherer was "vindicated," i.e., found right or made right, whereas the proud Pharisee was not (Luke 18:14). There is in the Gospels not a hint of "forensic" or "imputed" righteousness, certainly not that incomprehensible "transferred righteousness" (*übereignete Gerechtigkeit*) of which Conzelmann speaks.[14]

Acts employs the verb *dikaioun* only in ch. 13, vs. 38–39, and it seems to mean "to make free." It is closely related to forgiveness. The claim made is that in faith is accomplished what the law could not effect. The RSV so renders it: ". . . by him everyone that believes is freed from everything from which you could not be freed by the law of Moses." This may be the force of *dikaioun* in Rom. 6:7: "For he who has died is freed (*dedikaiōtai*) from sin" (RSV).

Paul employs the verb *dikaioun* in several letters, and its force is uniformly stronger than the idea of "counting right." There is no support for the idea of "counting right those who are not right." In Rom. 2:13 his usage is as unambiguous as it is significant: "For not the hearers of the law are justified ones (*dikaioi*) with God, but the doers of the law shall be justified (*dikaiōthēsontai*)." As in the Gospels (cf. Matt. 7:24; 12:50; Luke 10:28), there is a strong emphasis here upon doing. Actual compliance with the demands of the law is the requirement. The context is to the same effect, for God rewards each according to "his works" (Rom. 2:6), a sharp distinction being made between those "doing evil" (Rom. 2:9) and those "doing good" (Rom. 2:10). Significant too is the pairing of the adjective *dikaios* and the verb *dikaioun* in Rom. 2:13. The RSV renders the first "righteous" and the second "justified." The doers of the law, or those who do good, are "justified" in the sense that they are found righteous, not just counted righteous.

In Rom. 3:4 is a quotation of Ps. 51:4 in which the force of "justification" is inescapable, and it is not forensic: "In order that you may be justified in your words and that you may prevail when you are judged." The psalmist is confessing his own sin, and his concern is to set the record straight. He is wrong and God is right. When God speaks, he speaks the truth. When God is questioned or judged, God comes out victorious. Paul's application is in keeping with the thrust of the psalm. He affirms that

God is true and man false (Rom. 3:4a). He is not suggesting that God be merely "counted right," and it is unthinkable that he should mean that God is "counted righteous although not righteous." God is found right or proved right. This is what he means by "justification."

The interchange of *dikaios* ("just" or "righteous") with *dikaioun* (to "justify" or "find right") is found again in Rom. 3:10, 20. "There is not a righteous one (*dikaios*), not even one" (Rom. 3:10). The verses that follow (Rom. 3:11–18) show that it is actual sin which results in their not being *dikaios*, i.e., righteous. Forensic ideas are absent. Rom. 3:20 recapitulates: "Wherefore by the works of the law will nobody be justified [found righteous] before him." This preserves the idea of real righteousness, or its absence, in Ps. 143:2: "Enter not into judgment with thy servant; for no man living is righteous before thee."

The idea of acquittal, being found or proven right, is apparent in Rom. 8:33 f.: "God is the one justifying; who is the one condemning?" If God declares one right, who dares declare him wrong? The emphasis is upon vindication, or acquittal, and there is no necessary implication of "counting righteous those who are unrighteous." In I Cor. 4:4 "justified" clearly means "proven right." It reads, "I am not aware of anything against myself, but I am not thereby acquitted (*dedikaiōmai*)." He is not thus proven right or righteous. The context of I Cor. 6:11 indicates that actual righteousness is in Paul's thought as he reminds the readers of the nature of their salvation: "You were washed, you were sanctified, you were justified." He has just equated the *adikoi* ("unjust" or "unrighteous" ones) with fornicators, idolaters, adulterers, catamites, homosexuals, thieves, extortioners, drunkards, slanderers, and robbers (I Cor. 6:9 f.). Those who are "justified" (*edikaiōthēte*) are no longer characterized by these ugly things. Clearly, to Paul, "justification" is moral and existential, not forensic, or "as if." Bultmann, in English translation, happily renders *dikaioun* "rightwised," but he spoils it all by remaining bound to the Reformation idea of forensic righteousness.[15] Justification is "finding right," "proving right," or "making right." [16]

In I Tim. 3:16 it clearly means "to vindicate" or "find right" as applied to Jesus.

Paul does not credit righteousness in man to man's own works but to God's work. Putting man in the right or making him righteous is freely God's work (cf. Rom. 3:24, 26, 28, 30). Righteousness is received out of man's faith, not accomplished out of man's works (Gal. 3:8, 11; 5:4). Habakkuk 2:4 (Rom. 1:17; Gal. 3:11; Heb. 10:38) is best understood as affirming that the righteous man lives by faithfulness. The Hebrew text reads, "by his faithfulness," presumably man's faithfulness to God's covenant.[17] The Septuagint removes the ambiguity, changing "his" to "my," i.e., God's, faithfulness. In the New Testament adaptations, "faithfulness" is rendered *pistis,* normally "faith" but sometimes "faithfulness" (Rom. 3:3). Whether it is out of man's faith or out of faithfulness (man's or God's), the solid idea is that man does thus live and that a life thus lived is a righteous one. Probably the full underlying idea is that the righteous man lives out of faith in the faithfulness of God. But God's work is good work, making upright and not merely counting upright. This is affirmed in Gal. 2:16 f., where Paul denies that those "justified in Christ" are yet found to be the same old sinners. To be "justified" (Gal. 2:16 f.) is to be found or made "righteous" (Gal. 2:21). Paul's interchange between "justified" (Gal. 2:16 f.) and "righteousness" (Gal. 2:21) is significant. The RSV actually renders *dikaiosunē* as "justification" in v. 21. It would be better to render *dikaiōthēsetai* (Gal. 2:16 f.) "made righteous" and to retain "righteousness" in v. 21.

Titus 3:1–7 provides an excellent context for studying the full, rich idea of "justification." The author affirms that our salvation is God's free work, out of "the goodness and loving kindness of God our Savior" (Titus 3:4) and "not because of deeds done by us in righteousness, but in virtue of his own mercy" (Titus 3:5a). It is God's work of "regeneration and renewal in the Holy Spirit" (Titus 3:5b). It is to the end "that we might be justified by his grace" (Titus 3:7a). The overriding concern of the passage is to call for good deeds. There is the reminder of the old sinful ways which are no longer proper to the readers. "Justi-

fication" is God's provision for a new kind of existence in righteousness.

To conclude, all God's people are "saints"; they are "sanctified." They are not perfect nor sinless. Neither are they simply
"justified" in a forensic sense, counted righteous though not
righteous. God is not a bad judge who "fixes the ticket." He is a
righteous God who offers himself freely in making man righteous.
Though yet sinners, we are saints, being brought into conformity
with God's own goodness.

SINNERS IN NEED

We are sinners yet saints. We are saints yet sinners. In this
polarity and tension we find our existence under God. As sinners
open to God's mercy, we dare not deny what already God has
done for us in accepting us though we are not in our own right
acceptable (Tillich) and in opening up to us his resources for our
renewal. As saints we dare not forget that we are yet sinners,
moving homeward but not yet home. Man at best in his historical
existence is a person divinely addressed, called to decision and
pilgrimage, one who "stands beneath the sign of exodus" and
whose "horizon is hope." [18]

None Sinless. The dogmatic position of some scholars that
there is no good in man is matched by the equally absurd position
of others that they are sinless. This is no new heresy. I John
devotes much of its space to refuting the claim of some that they
were without sin. John is blunt. He says categorically, "If we say
that we have not sin, we deceive ourselves and the truth is not
in us" (I John 1:8). Further, "If we say that we have not sinned,
we make him [God] a liar and his word is not in us" (I John
1:10). It is to falsify God, fool ourselves, and incarnate a lie for
one to boast that he is sinless. This holds for "saints" as well as
for "sinners."

On the surface, John seems to contradict himself, for he makes
strong claims which seem to say that a Christian does not sin:
"Whoever abides in him [Christ] sins not; whoever sins has not

seen him, nor known him" (I John 3:6) Again, "Whoever is begotten of God does not do sin, because his seed abides in him, and he cannot sin, because he is begotten of God" (I John 3:9). Do contradictory claims lie next to one another unreconciled in the same letter? It is incredible that a writer would so radically contradict himself on a main point of his letter. The statements can be reconciled, in part in terms of Greek usage and in part in terms of the historical situation to which John is speaking.

Greek tenses may be appealed to as somewhat relieving the apparent contradictions, but this is to be done with caution, for the author was not a scientific grammarian writing with grammars and lexicons spread around him.[19] Biblical writers were capable of making deliberate distinctions through choice of tenses or otherwise, but they, as we, could use the same tenses or other grammatical forms interchangeably. (Cf. our precise and also loose use of "shall" and "will," "may" and "can," etc.) But in I John, some weight probably may be placed upon shift in tenses. In I John 1:8 the present tense (*hamartian ouk echomen*) is used: "We have not sin." In I John 1:10 the perfect (*ouch hēmartēkamen*) is used: "We have not sinned." John rejects as false any claim that one has no sin in his present or past.

In I John 3:6 the present tense is used again with respect to sinning, and the translation may best be as follows: "Everyone abiding in him does not go on sinning; everyone who goes on sinning has not seen him nor has he known him." (Greek places the negative with the verb, where English prefers to put it with the subject.) It is to be admitted that the Greek "present" tense can be punctiliar, i.e., represent an action as singular, but more often it is linear or continuous.[20] So interpreted here, John is not denying the occurrence of sin in a Christian life, but he is denying that it can go on unchecked, as normative. The same tense usage occurs in I John 3:9, and probably John's intention is to say, "Everyone who has been begotten of God does not go on doing (*ou poiei*) sin, because his seed abides in him; and he is not able to go on sinning (*hamartanein*), because he has been begotten of God." [21]

A more solid case can be made from the perspective of the

historical situation with which John is concerned. Apparently there were those who identified themselves as Christians who claimed to have "the light," to be in the Spirit, and to be sinless. Either they were Gnostics or had striking affinities with what later emerges as a form of gnosticism.[22] These people apparently worked with a dualism which viewed all that is material, including the flesh, as evil and only spirit as good. They rejected or explained away the humanity of Christ, and they saw their own true existence as being in the world of light and spirit. They claimed to be sinless and probably to be above sin. John flatly rejects this claim (I John 1:8, 10). At the same time these people were living a life far below their lofty claims, presumably justifying it on the claim that for those "in the Spirit," the life lived in the flesh was unimportant. Gnostic dualism could lead to either asceticism or license. The ascetics said that the material was evil and was to be shunned. This resulted in celibacy, abstinence from certain foods, etc. Others rationalized the matter, saying that their higher life in the Spirit exempted them from ordinary demands at the level of the flesh. They were the libertines or antinomians. John rejects this rationale. He sees all life as of one piece, not to be so divided.

The major thrust of I John is to reject Gnostic dualism and insist upon the wholeness of life. John begins by affirming a real incarnation. God's kind of existence entered history and flesh so tangibly that it could be seen, heard, and felt with hands (I John 1:1–3). He also argued that "truth" must be embodied. It is something done, not just believed (I John 1:6). So also, love is to be incarnated. One who does not love his brother, to the point of martyrdom or in giving another his daily material needs, does not really know God and does not really love (I John 3: 15–18).

To sum up, John rejects the high claim to sinlessness (I John 1:8, 10), and he demonstrates the absurdity and fallacy of high claims and low living. One is not sinless, but neither can the children of light or those abiding in Christ go on living the same old life. We are saints but also sinners, but we are not the same old unrestrained sinners. We are living in the tension of "saints yet sinners," already having been delivered from the tyranny of sin yet having to continue the battle with sin.

This tension is made vivid in I John 2:1. John says, "My children, these things I write in order that you may not sin (*hamartēte*)." The goal is sinless perfection, and nothing short of this is proper as a goal. But he continues the sentence in saying, "but if one should sin, we have a Paraclete with the Father, Jesus Christ the righteous one." The goal is sinlessness but the possibility and the actuality is that of sin. The ideal is that we walk (i.e., live) as Jesus walked (I John 2:6). We are called to this kind of existence and Christ himself is our hope and help for such existence. Already we are the children of God and ultimately we shall be like Jesus, for we shall one day see him as he really is (I John 3:2). This is the horizon of our hope, and in view of this, one is to "sanctify himself [be holy] just as that one is holy" (I John 3:3).

The Need of Forgiveness. To forgive and be forgiven belongs properly and necessarily to the saints, who are yet sinners. Forgiving and being forgiven belong together. To be unforgiving is to remain unforgiven, precisely because to be unforgiving is to be unforgivable. Jesus taught that if we do not forgive men their trespasses, the heavenly Father will not forgive us (Matt. 6:15). This is not arbitrary. It is not that God is unwilling to forgive the unforgiving but that they are unable to receive. A door closed is closed from both directions. A heart closed to others is blocked both ways.

The point is graphic in Luke 6:37, "Release (*apoluete*) and you shall be released (*apoluthēsesthe*)." The RSV captures the intention in its rendering, "Forgive, and you will be forgiven," but this obscures the fact that the word actually describes a freeing or releasing. To be unforgiving is to remain bound. In binding others, one binds himself whether by unforgivingness or otherwise. It is like holding a tiger by the tail; man and tiger are caught. One cannot release the tiger without risk, and one cannot forgive without risk; but forgive one must.

There is a proper place for forgetting in forgiving, but it is second and not first. It follows but does not precede. It may be well to forgive and forget, but one cannot forget and thus forgive. To forgive one must first remember. Simply to forget is negative; it changes nothing. Simply to forget ignores the needs of the offender, and it drives the sense of having been wronged deep into one's own being where resentment does its greatest damage. Simply to forget without forgiving is indulgence. Forgiveness is positive and creative, cleansing both offender and offended: indulgence is negative.[23]

It is not only necessary to remember before one can forgive and forget, but offender and offended must remember together.[24] They first must remember together, look at the wrong together, condemn it together, and they may forget together. Only thus may one gain his brother (Matt. 18:15). In this remembering together/forgiving/forgetting, each gains the other. It does not follow that forgetting is the last word in forgiving. Sometimes precisely because one forgives he has no right to forget.[25] To forgive is to assume new responsibility—for the rehabilitation of the offender and for restitution where damage has been done. Forgiving is not the end of the matter. It may be a giant step in a new creative relationship which continues in new directions and which issues in new dimensions of life.

Saints are yet sinners. Sinners require forgiveness. Sinners require the reciprocity of forgiving and being forgiven.

Cleansing. Forgiveness is itself a form of cleansing, but cleansing goes beyond forgiving. This is why one cannot forgive by forgetting and why forgetting does not always properly follow forgiving. The care of souls is the proper work of all the saints, however dependent for guidance they may be upon those who specialize in "the care of souls." Jesus placed this burden upon all his followers. He dramatized it on the night of his betrayal through the washing of his disciples' feet (John 13:1–17). He left for us an example and a commission which sinner-saints dare not forget nor neglect.

"Foot washing" is practiced by various Christian bodies, but it is ignored by most Christians. The Roman Church observes it chiefly through its hierarchy, and some Baptist and other groups observe it congregationally. At least they take seriously the injunction of Jesus, whether with adequate understanding of his intention or not. Most Christians, not satisfied or comfortable with its literal observance, ignore the whole matter. But dare we leave it thus? John gives precious space to this narrative, even though each subject selected required the exclusion of others from his book (John 20:30 f.; 21:25). He must have counted it of great importance. Jesus devoted considerable time and attention to the matter on the night of his betrayal, when time with his disciples was running out. All his words are precious. Surely this act and words from his last hours before Golgotha are too significant to be left alone.

What is the heart of the matter? What did Jesus mean when he said, "You also ought to wash one another's feet" (John 13: 14)? Clues abound in the passage, and they point to something far beyond a physical act of foot washing.

The first clue is in John 13:7: "What I am doing you do not understand just now, but you will understand after these things." There was nothing new or mysterious about washing one another's feet as such. This was a common practice. Open sandals and dusty paths meant that feet were soon soiled, however clean they may have been when one left his home. At formal dinners Jewish people reclined on couches. They did not sit with feet concealed under the table. The feet extended outward from the table in plain view of all. It was customary for the host to provide for the washing of his guests' feet. But when Jesus washed his disciples' feet, more was intended than is obvious in the familiar act itself. John 13:7 hints at symbolism yet to be interpreted. The whole Gospel of John builds heavily upon "signs," acted parables.

A further clue appears in John 13:8: "If I do not wash you, you have no part with me." More than a physical act is implied, although the simple, physical act may embody or symbolize that something. The strongest clues are in John 13:10, "The one having been bathed (*leloumenos*) has not need except to have his feet washed (*nipsasthai*), but he is cleansed (*katharos*) wholly; and you are cleansed ones (*katharoi*), yet not all of you are." There is an obvious play on the words rendered "bathed" and "washed." There is something like a full bath which requires no repetition. It is done "once for all." There are subsequent acts which are like the washing of feet, required repeatedly. Presumably, Jesus referred first to the initial and decisive experience of conversion, unique and permanently valid. But beyond this, the saints are yet sinners and require daily cleansing. Our "feet" are soiled and require "washing" day after day.

This interpretation is strengthened by the occurrence of the term "cleansed" (*katharos*) in John 13:10. This refers to more than physical sanitation; it has basic religious usage. The point becomes conclusive when it is said that all of the disciples there were "cleansed," except one. Jesus referred to Judas (John 13:11). Surely, Judas' problem was not that he had failed to take a bath before leaving for the Last Supper. Judas had not been "bathed." He needed more than "foot washing." He needed the initial experience of conversion. The others needed only the further ministry of "foot washing."

It is to be observed that equal stress is laid upon washing another's feet and allowing him to wash our feet. Peter must accept this ministry for himself (John 13:8). Each must wash the other's feet (John 13:14). Just as we must both forgive and accept forgiveness, so must we "wash" and be "washed." This is the continuing "care of souls" which belongs necessarily to the life of sinner-saints. With forgiveness there must be cleansing. By "washing one another's feet" Jesus seems to mean that we owe it to one another to help one another with our sin problems. It requires the same honesty and humility to offer it as to receive it, to receive it as to offer it. Thus it must be for saints who are yet sinners.

Chapter 7

SALVATION
AS GIFT AND DEMAND

Of the many paradoxes in the New Testament, one of the more striking and persistent is that of salvation as God's gift and God's demand. The Germans, with a love for play on words, bring it to focus in the phrase *Gabe und Aufgabe* ("gift and task"). Salvation is thus bipolar in that on the one side it is God's free gift, beyond the reach of man's virtue or achievement; yet on the other hand it requires everything of us, placing us under most radical demand. It is free and costs everything!

Neither Legalism Nor Libertinism

Religion has the unhappy lot to tend to fall victim either to legalism or to antinomian libertinism. Legalism is not identical with law. Laws may be natural, like gravitation, or formal, like rules. They may derive from nature, custom, or arbitrary ruling. Legalism is the goal of compliance with law for its own sake. Once conformity to law for the sake of reward becomes one's ultimate goal, the next step is to bring that law within one's reach. This results in the reduction of law to rules and regulations which may be managed, where achievements may be outwardly observed, "graded," and publicized. It opens the way to casuistry, the legal fiction of providing technical loopholes in laws so that one may "comply" without undue cost. During the Lenten season a grocery chain offered a substitute for the forbidden meat and called it "Lent without a letdown." The Pharisaic ruling that to swear by the altar is not binding but to swear by the gold on the altar is binding (Matt. 23:18) was a legalistic fiction calculated to favor the informed and victimize the uninformed. Legalism is the practice of avoiding the demand of a law without becoming unlawful, remaining within the letter of the law without meeting its intention. The maneuvering to achieve that end is casuistry. Tax shelters and loopholes which make it possible for millionaires to pay no income tax while the masses of people suffer under the burden of taxation is but one example of a legalism which is legally "right" but morally and ethically wrong.

Religion is legalistic whenever it measures itself by rules and regulations which may be checked off and graded: Sabbath laws, food laws, "do's" and "don'ts" in social behavior, etc. This is not to deny a rightful place to regulations. Health without diet is impossible, for there are laws of health that belong to nature and not to arbitrary ruling. Laws regulating speed limits can save innocent lives. So it is with mental health, with a healthy family relationship or community relationship. Laws belong properly to life, but legalism is something else. It becomes its worst when it becomes religious. The Judaizers of Paul's day who made so much of circumcision were legalists. So were those whom James censored, substituting creedal confession of God for looking after the needs of widows, orphans, the hungry, and the men who worked their fields (James 1:26 f.; 2:14–17, 19; 5:1–6).

Libertinism is the opposite of legalism. It is antinomian (*nomos* is Greek for "law"). It declares its freedom from all rules and regulations. It may justify itself by appeal to "nature." In secular expression it claims that the purpose of life is to live. One should follow out his biological destiny: eat when hungry, drink when thirsty, etc. In gnosticism its argument was that only the higher self of spirit or soul is the true self, hence the action of the body is indifferent. While the "soul" or "spirit" enjoys its higher life, the body is free to follow its own laws.

Paul found it necessary to fight on two fronts, against the

legalism of the Judaizers and against the libertinism of some of his own followers.[1] The legalist stressed circumcision, food laws, and the observance of special days, weeks, and seasons (Gal. 4:8–11; 6:12). The libertines argued that since salvation is the gift of God's grace, we are free. Their cry was, "All things are lawful," but they failed to see that such "freedom" could be a new form of bondage (I Cor. 6:12). Appealing to nature, they held to the proverb "Foods for the stomach and the stomach for foods" (I Cor. 6:13). Some so rationalized the matter that they convinced themselves that the only way to serve God is by sinning. Since saving is God's work, one serves God's glory, they reasoned, by giving him yet more sin from which to save us. Apparently it was this fallacy which Paul was refuting in his letter to the Romans: "What then shall we say? Shall we continue in sin that grace may abound?" (Rom. 6:1). Some preachers to this day can be heard decrying social reform and all good works as "deceptions of the devil." In their perverted doctrine, all man's goodness is really evil. Like the Corinthian Gnostics, they would have us continue in sin (social injustice) that grace might abound.

The ever-present problem in religion is to escape both legalism and libertinism. How can one be morally and ethically responsible without becoming legalistic? How can one enter into the freedom granted by God's grace without becoming an antinomian libertine? How can one live in open goodness without ostentation? It is this narrow, anguished way which is most elusive. It was to this way that Jesus called men of old (Matt. 7:13–14). The gate is narrow, the road is tortuous, and the fellow travelers are few, but the end result is life. This is a way into which one does not drift. It must be entered, deliberately. The gate leading to death is wide enough—wide enough to include legalism and/or libertinism. It is wide enough that one may drift into it without knowing it and be swept on by the crowd to the inauthentic existence which is death. But to enter the narrow gate and walk with the few the way that leads to life is possible to decision alone. One must deliberately enter that gate. To walk the way that is neither legalistic nor libertine is a possibility only to anguished choice and commitment.

In the New Testament, possibly it is the Gospel of Matthew that most forcefully combats both legalism and libertinism,[2] although this was a recurring problem for Paul (I Corinthians, Galatians, and Romans especially). Matthew seems to have written some time after the first Jewish-Roman war (A.D. 66–70) at a time when the break between Judaism and Christianity (synagogue and church) was almost final but when the two were yet sufficiently in touch with one another to engage in painful controversy.[3] Pharisaic Judaism at Jamnia and elsewhere was trying to rebuild the nation around the Law. In process was the codification and development of the tradition which eventually emerged as the Mishna and later, in fuller form, the Babylonian and Palestinian Talmuds (each Talmud built upon the one Mishna). But Matthew had also to fight on another front, possibly more difficult. Within the church was the threat of antinomianism, the reduction of salvation to gift without demand, to hearing without heeding. Hence Matthew's strong emphasis throughout on "doing" and upon obedience. One thinks, for example, of the parable of the two foundations with their emphasis upon doing which closes the Sermon on the Mount (Matt. 7:24–27), the description of the last judgment (cf. Matt., ch. 25), and the Great Commission with its stress upon obedience (Matt. 28:20).

W. D. Davies in his *Setting of the Sermon on the Mount* has thrown a flood of light on the Matthean sermon, especially in terms of perspective from which to see it. Actually, his book offers keys to the study of the whole Gospel of Matthew. He develops the point that God's demands are always preceded by his mercies; e.g., God acted in mercy to deliver the Israelites from Egyptian bondage before he gave the law at Mt. Sinai. So, the heavy demands of the Sermon on the Mount are given in a setting of mercy. Jesus "went about in all Galilee, teaching in their synagogues and preaching the gospel of the kingdom and healing every sickness and disease among the people" (Matt. 4:23). This picture of mercy is the immediate background to the Sermon (Matt., chs. 5 to 7). Immediately following are various merciful acts (Matt., chs. 8 to 9); cleansing a leper, healing many people, calming a storm, healing Gadarene demoniacs, healing a paralytic, healing a woman of her hemorrhage, raising to life a ruler's daughter, healing two blind men, and healing a deaf man. The threefold ministry of teaching, preaching, and healing is restated at the close of this section (Matt. 9:35), just as it appeared just before the sermon (Matt. 4:23). The sermon with its heavy, almost crushing, moral-ethical demand is, indeed, in a setting of mercy.

Free, Yet It Costs Everything

Where the Spirit of the Lord is, there is freedom (II Cor. 3:17), and it is for freedom that Christ frees us (Gal. 5:1). But freedom itself is not free; it costs. It costs to gain it and it costs to keep it. Salvation is freedom; it is more but it is that. Paradoxically, it is free yet costs everything. Salvation is the gift of God (Eph. 2:8),[4] his creative workmanship (Eph. 2:10). The grace of God and his free gift in grace abound to sinners who may freely receive (Rom. 5:15). Christian generosity has its roots in God's generosity, to whom be thanks "for his inexpressible gift!" (II Cor. 9:15). Our whole "calling" is "according to the measure of Christ's free gift" (Eph. 4:7). Salvation is indeed "the heavenly gift" (Heb. 6:4). The promise of him who is "the Alpha and the Omega" is that to the thirsty he "will give freely from the fountain of the water of life" (Rev. 21:6). The New Testament Apocalypse brings the New Testament's message to a fitting conclusion in the invitation: "The Spirit and the bride say, Come! and let the one hearing say, Come! and let the one who thirsts come; let the one who wishes take the water of life freely!" (Rev. 22:17). The Christian ministry is to be built upon the principle, "Freely ye received; freely give" (Matt. 10:8).

Salvation in no sense rests upon man's merit or man's work. It is the free gift of God's grace. In this sense it is a "come and get it" salvation. But there is another side, equally important. There is a sense in which it is not a "come and get it" salvation.

Paradoxically the salvation which is authentic and meaningful costs everything. The price is not an arbitrary tag affixed to the commodity by the merchant. It is cost which is built into salvation, inherent in it and inseparable from it. There is a real sense in which salvation means that one must die to live, give to receive, lose to win (contrary to the popular wit: "I can't win for losing"). One must surrender all if he would follow Jesus (Mark 8:34).

There are parables which point to the bipolar nature of salvation as gift and demand. The parable of the seed growing by itself points to the gift (Mark 4:26–29). True, the explicit subject is the kingdom of God and not salvation, but the kingdom of God is discussed as it bears upon salvation. It is under the rule of God that the kind of life which is "salvation" is possible. In the parable of the growing seed, it is the mystery and dynamic of life which is marveled at. The stages of growth may be observed, from the first blade to the ripened grain, but the sprouting of life itself is beyond our understanding. Life is there within the seed, as something given. The farmer can only cooperate with its nature, watch and wait. So it is with God's kingdom. It is and it comes, out of its own dynamic and not out of the "Messianic" wars of the Zealots nor the strivings of men otherwise.[5]

The cost side of the kingdom and of the salvation which it provides is stressed in the parables of the hidden treasure and the pearl of great price (Matt. 13:44–46). To gain the treasure found in the field, one will sell all that he has to buy the field (Matt. 13:44). For the pearl of surpassing value, he will sell his connoisseur's collection of beautiful pearls. It must be remembered that his were not paste pearls. He was a merchant who had been looking for "beautiful pearls" (Matt. 13:45).

Salvation may entail one's turning from the hog pens and hunger in a foreign land as with the prodigal son (Luke 15:12–24), but this is not the complete picture nor the most significant one. After all, it should not be surprising that a hungry, friendless boy would give up the disillusionments and disappointments of the foreign land for the security of home. But salvation also includes the giving up of "treasures" and "precious pearls" for the kingdom. It may mean forsaking one's boat and father to follow Jesus (Mark 1:20). It may cost one his family and friends (Mark 3:31–35). It may mean bondage and martyrdom (John 21:18 f.).

THE KINGDOM FOR THE POOR

It is a striking thing about the preaching of Jesus that he made the kingdom of God central in his preaching and related it primarily to the poor: "Blessed are the poor, for yours is the kingdom of God" (Luke 6:20). Again: "Fear not, little flock, for your father is pleased to give you the kingdom" (Luke 12:32). The poor, the helpless, the disinherited are given the kingdom of God! Here is paradox, not only in that contrary to ancient expectations the kingdom is given to the poor, but in that the kingdom itself proves to be paradoxical, both gift and demand.

Jesus did not create the concept of the kingdom of God. This was a concept familiar to ancient Israel. The term is secure in the Old Testament, usually referring to the kingship of God. *Malkut* in the Old Testament almost always stands for government, authority, the power of a king, and only rarely for a realm in a spatial sense, a territory.[6] The kingdom of God is the reign of God, which is "neither a spatial nor a static concept; it is a *dynamic concept,*" the fulfillment of a righteous reign, constantly longed for but never fulfilled through earthly kings or kingdoms.[7] As God's achievement it is his gift; as God's righteous rule, it is his demand.

What is most striking in Jesus' proclamation of the kingdom of God is that it was related directly and primarily to "the poor." Who are the blessed poor to whom is given the kingdom (Luke 6:20)? They are the *'amme ha ares,* "the people of the land." They are "the uneducated, the ignorant, whose *religious* ignorance and *moral* behavior stand in the way of their access to salvation, according to the convictions of the time."[8] Jesus knew them as "the poor" (Luke 6:20), those who "labor and are heavy laden" (Matt. 11:28).

In Matt. 5:3 they are "the poor in Spirit," but Luke's shorter form, "the poor," is probably original (Luke 6:20). Elsewhere, speaking of the same people, both Matthew (Matt. 11:5) and Luke (Luke 7:22) speak of them simply as "the poor." Luke's form preserves the original emphasis upon actual poverty, but Matthew's version is true in interpretation. Although "the poor" included little people who were actually poor in material things, "the poor" also included some whose "poverty" was not material, like the "taxgatherers and sinners" (Mark 2:16; Matt. 11:19). These were people excluded from the synagogue either because of moral charges or simply because they engaged in despised trades which were thought to defile them. They were to Jesus "the little ones" (Mark 9:42; Matt. 10:42; 18:10, 14); they were "the simple ones" or "babes" (*nēpioi*); they were "the least ones" (Matt. 25: 40, 45).

In Synoptic tradition, there is strong emphasis upon the poor as the recipients of the good news. Jeremias sees the stamp of primitiveness in the two-beat rhythm (in the Greek text) of Matt. 11:5 and its parallel in Luke 7:22: "The blind see, the lame walk, the lepers are cleansed, the deaf hear, the dead are raised, the poor hear the good news." This early saying stands behind Matthew and Luke, and it is an adaptation and combination of Isa. 35:5 ff.; 29:18 f.; and 61:1 f. It celebrates the time of salvation, good news for "the poor" who include the helpless and dispossessed. Jesus incarnated and actualized this vision from Isaiah. It was this which was his reply to the question of John the Baptist, "Are you the coming one, or shall we look for another?" (Matt. 11:3; and Luke 7:20).

It is significant that when he thus described his mission he also gave what is probably the most neglected beatitude in the New Testament, "And blessed is he who is not scandalized by me" (Matt. 11:6; Luke 7:23). Why would this offend or scandalize anyone? Precisely, because this did not conform to current Messianic understandings. This did not conform to the concept of the kingdom of God as vindication of the righteous people of the nation Israel in its struggle against such alien powers as the Roman Empire. Instead of leading the armies of the Zealots in battle against Rome and instead of rewarding the "righteous" observers of the Law, Jesus directed his ministry to the outcasts, the harlots, the taxgatherers, the sick, the helpless, and all who knew their need and responded with childlike trust. Jesus' ministry was especially offensive because it was offered "the poor" who included "sinners." Jeremias accounts for the reaction to Jesus' ministry to "the poor":

> The good news was a slap in the face to all the religious feelings of the time. The supreme religious duty for contemporary Judaism was to keep away from sinners. Table fellowship in Qumran was open to the pure, to the full members.[9]

Contempt for the common people, "the people of the land," is reflected in the retort, "This crowd, which does not know the law, are accursed ones!" (John 7:49).

In Nazareth, where Jesus grew up, he once preached in the synagogue on a Sabbath (Luke 4:16–30). He read from Isaiah (Isa. 61:1 f.; cf. 58:6), indicating his understanding of his own mission. The emphasis, as elsewhere, is upon the good news for the poor, release for captives, sight for the blind, liberty for the oppressed, and "the acceptable year of the Lord," presumably the jubilee year, a fiftieth year when each captive was freed to return to his family and property (Lev. 25:8–17). Chiefly it is the good news of God's dynamic action in behalf of the helpless.

Salvation, then, is God's gift and his demand. It is the new kind of existence made possible under his sovereign rule, the kingdom of God. It is sight for the blind, hearing for the deaf, cleansing for the lepers, strength for the weak, life for the dead, liberty for captives. It is gift, for these can only receive. They cannot achieve. But it is also demand. The kingdom of God is God's righteous reign. The good news is not that God simply rewrites the account books, balancing them in our favor. He does not just count righteous those who are not righteous. It is real sight, hearing, cleansing, freedom, and life that he gives. It is also such existence that he requires. He gives what he demands, and he also demands of us that we live the new life which he gives.

The poor are given the kingdom; they cannot earn it. But the kingdom is demand. Paul undercut all libertine and antinomian understandings of the kingdom in saying, "For the kingdom of God is not eating and drinking, but righteousness and peace and joy in the Holy Spirit" (Rom. 14:17). Neglected in the study of Pauline soteriology is his stern warning:

> Do you know that the unrighteous shall not inherit the kingdom of God? Do not fool yourselves; neither fornicators, nor idolaters, nor adulterers, nor catamites, nor homosexuals, nor thieves, nor greedy people, nor drunkards, nor slanderers, nor robbers, shall inherit the kingdom of God. (I Cor. 6:9 f.; cf. Gal. 5:21; Eph. 5:5.)

Paul knew the kingdom as gift, as inheritance; and he knew that God saves sinners. But he did not know a forensic "justification." God saves sinners, but it is with a salvation that demands a new kind of life.

THE EASY YOKE

In one of the tenderest expressions of Jesus' concern for the "little people" is the blending of gift and demand:

> Come to me, all of you who labor and who are burdened down, and I will refresh you. Take my yoke upon you and learn from me, for I am gentle and humble in heart, and you shall find rest for your souls; for my yoke is easy and my burden is light. (Matt. 11:28–30.)

The "babes" (*nēpioi*) or "little people" to whom this is addressed are contrasted with "the wise and understanding" (Matt. 11:25). Behind this is the idea, rejected by Jesus, that the piety which God respects is that of religious knowledge and cultic conformity.

Piety as thus understood was bound up with cultic practice centered in the shrines. Our English terms "pagan" and "heathen" preserve this fallacy; for to those who coined the terms, a "pagan" was one who lived in a village (*pagus* in Latin), and the "heathen" were those who lived in the "heath," i.e., in the country. The people of piety were those in the cities and towns which had shrines and cultic centers. The people of the villages were "peasants" or "pagans," and those in the country heaths were "heathen." Even the term "villain" (from *villa,* "village" or "farmhouse") reflects the city orientation of ancient religion with its suspicion of or contempt for villagers and rural people.

Bound up with this idea of piety was that of religious knowledge as knowledge of the laws of religion. The Pharisees made the study of the Torah central to their concern, and they despised the "ignorant" as ungodly. To them one ignorant of the law could not be pious, for piety required scrupulous observance of the Sabbath, food laws, purification rites, etc. The attitude of the Pharisees expressed in John 7:49 is not an isolated one: "But this crowd, who know not the law, are accursed ones."

Jesus not only championed "the babes" over against "the wise and understanding," but he indicated that the knowledge which matters most is not that of the scholar but that belonging to faith. Saving knowledge is not knowledge of facts but knowledge of God: "This is eternal life, that they should know thee, the only true God, and Jesus Christ whom thou hast sent" (John 17:3). God's revelation of himself is not to the scholars who excel but to the little people who trust (I Cor. 1:21). This is not to discredit scholarship as such, but it is to say that factual knowledge is not itself saving. It is better to be an "egghead" than just an "egg," but being an "egghead" is not enough.

The modern counterpart to the Pharisaic fallacy which confused religious learning with piety is the fallacy which presumes to think that what God most esteems is creedal orthodoxy. The Pharisees were real scholars. Their mistake was that they placed too much emphasis upon the externals of the law, especially in their cultic expression. Today, we may witness the strange phenomenon of some who despise learning yet stake their hopes upon their own brand of intellectualism, even if it be no more than a barren and misinformed "orthodoxy."

"Yoke" was a term used figuratively in Jesus' time for the study of the Law. One took on "the yoke of the Law" when he

entered into serious study of it. Jesus offered discipleship with a
different emphasis. It was not that Jesus was indifferent to Torah.
He was not. He came not to destroy it but to fulfill it (Matt.
5:17). That is, he came to interpret the heart or intention of
"the Law and the Prophets" and also to incarnate that intention.
The six "antitheses" of the Matthean Sermon on the Mount
(Matt. 5:21–48) illustrate what Jesus meant by not destroying
but rather fulfilling the Law and the Prophets: not mere external
compliance but taking into the depths of one's person the intention of the Law. The three illustrations of piety in Matt. 6:1–18
(almsgiving, prayer, and fasting) serve further to illustrate the
primacy of attitude, disposition, and purpose in piety. This kind
of piety may be instructed by scholarship, but the piety itself
comes from knowing God himself. This knowledge is possible
only to that faith which is the openness of trust.

Jesus invited the little people who were struggling under the
pressures of life to come under his "yoke," his discipleship, with
the assurance that it would prove to be not a new burden but
a lift. It would be that which refreshes. His yoke is not a set of
arbitrary rules, as in cultic religion. Rather, his "yoke" is the
discipline or discipleship suited to our nature and needs. His yoke
is "easy." The word "easy" translates *chrēstos,* which may also
be rendered "kind." It occurs in I Cor. 13:4, "Love is kind
(*chrēsteuetai*)." Christ's yoke is one that fits. His "burden" is
"light" (*elaphron*). It gives gladness.

It would be grossly unfair to Pharisaism to overlook its own
joy in the observance of the Law (cf. Ps. 1; 19; 119). Many
counted it sheer joy to meditate upon the Law day and night as
well as to try to comply with its intention. But when we read
extensively in the Talmud we observe the extent to which much
of this devotion resulted in preoccupation with the trivia of
cultic life. Judaism has a history of great peaks, decline, and
reform. This is abundantly clear in "the Law and the Prophets,"
where reform and new life are asserted from within Judaism.
Jesus was a Jew calling his own people back to the authenticity
of their own piety.

Jesus said that his "yoke" was easy and his "burden" light.

It was free of all externalism, artificiality, and arbitrariness. He did require acceptance of a yoke and a burden. There is demand in the salvation which he gives. But his yoke itself is a gift. It is the yoke which belongs properly, essentially, and happily to our existence. It means that in calling us to his discipline (discipleship), he is calling us to our own authentic existence, for salvation is becoming a true human being, nothing more and nothing less.

Goodness Without Ostentation

How can one live in open goodness without ostentation? How can one do alms, prayer, and fasting in secret and yet let his good works be seen of men to the glory of God? In the Sermon on the Mount it is precisely to this paradoxical stance that one is called. The tension is there and unrelieved.

> Ye are the light of the world. . . . Let your light so shine before men that they may see your good works and glorify your father who is in heaven. (Matt. 5:14, 16.)

> Take heed not to do your righteousness before men to be seen by them, otherwise ye have no reward with your father in heaven. (Matt. 6:1.)

We are the "salt of the earth" and "the light of the world," and it belongs essentially and necessarily to our salvation and our commission to be just that in the world, openly so. At the same time the meaningfulness of it all for us requires that it not be for show.

Under the analogies of "salt" and "light" Jesus indicated our necessary nature and function. If his, we are "salt." It is not that being his we should be "salt," but that unless we are "salt" we are not his. Under the other analogy, we are "the light of the world." A city that is built upon a mountain cannot be hidden. So it is with the light that is given us. It cannot be hidden. Jesus did not say that man should not light a lamp and then hide it under a basket or a bed. He said that men do not do that.

Unless one wants to burn the house down, he would never do that. Men light lamps to give light within the house. They place the lighted lamp upon a stand in order to enhance its light. So it is with God. He lights his lamps and places them in positions suited to give light to all in the house.

If we are the light of the world it is not because we are that of ourselves. Left to ourselves we are darkness. It is only as God's light is given us that we become light. God gives his light but with his gift of light comes demand—that it be shared with others. It is God's light to give, and the placing of his lighted lamps is likewise his prerogative. It is our proper function to let our God-given light shine to God's glory and to men's good. This is to be done openly and honestly. In other words, you were called to live in open goodness before God and men, "that they may see your good works" (Matt. 5:16).

In Matt. 6:1–8 there is not a contradiction to Matt. 5:13–16, but there is a necessary complement. The crux of the matter is the matter of motive. Our "good works" must be so done as to be seen of men, yet "to be seen of men" must not be the motive for our righteousness. To parade our almsgiving, prayers, or fasting before others in order to be seen is to rob religious practice of authenticity. One may be tempted to give, pray, or fast to be seen of men, or of God, or of oneself. One might keep secret from men his religious practice, but there is no way to keep it secret from God or oneself. Hence the peril remains. One may put on a show for God or for oneself as well as for other people, and with the same invalidation of the whole practice. Ultimately, then, what one calls his "good works," his "righteousness," or his "piety" will be exposed to many eyes. What is to be determined is not whether or not there will be observers but what is the quality of that to be observed. Its quality in turn, authentic or sham, is bound up with motive, whether for one's own glory and gain or for the glory of God and the good of men.

Salvation is not easy. It is gift but also awesome demand. It is acceptance of one's acceptance on the ground of God's goodness and not our own. It is the openness of faith to the resources of God for a new kind of existence. It is also commitment to the kind of life that means loving our enemies, turning the other cheek, going the second mile, and living in open goodness before God, before other people, and before ourselves—without the vitiating motive of selfish advantage.

"Freely ye received; freely give" (Matt. 10:8). Have fellowship (*koinōnia*) in "giving and receiving" (Phil. 4:15). There is the gift of mercy, "Have mercy upon me the sinner" (Luke 18:13), and the demand for perfection, "Be ye perfect as your father in heaven is perfect" (Matt. 5:48). This is our calling. This is the salvation which is gift and demand. In the tension of this polarity we are to have our existence.

Chapter 8

SELF DENIED
YET AFFIRMED

Paradox is truth too big for simple statement. To be an authentic person in Biblical perspective requires much that appears to be contradictory. Every credible student of the New Testament recognizes that at the heart of its claim is the demand that one must "deny himself" to follow Christ. This is the *sine qua non* of discipleship. Not only is it "no cross, no crown" but "no self-denial, no salvation." But embedded as deeply in the New Testament and the Old is another primary truth. One must affirm himself. One must love himself. Deny self; affirm self. Hate self; love self. Within this polarity alone is there salvation, authentic existence, fulfillment as a human being.[1]

"If anyone wishes to follow me, let him deny himself and take up his cross and follow me" (Mark 8:34). These are the terms for Christian discipleship. This in the New Testament is not negotiable. But more. Jesus also said, "I came that they may have life and that they may have it in abundance" (John 10:10). This promise of abundant life is our charter. The cross is its cost (Mark 8:34).[2] As to the summation of all God's law, that upon which it hangs, it is the commandment that one love God with his whole being (Mark 12:29 f., quoting Deut. 6:4 f.). But alongside the love for God is the love for one's neighbor, and the measure of that is "as one loves himself" (Mark 12:31). This not only permits and legitimates self-love; it catapults it into the central message of Scripture. Alongside the word "Deny thyself" is the equally strong "Love thyself."

DENY THYSELF

The centrality of Jesus' teaching that one must deny himself as the absolute condition for discipleship (Matt. 16:24; Mark 8:34; Luke 9:23) is much easier to demonstrate than it is to clarify the meaning of this demand. What is it to deny oneself? The meaning is not in the word itself, for it is used several ways, as both good and evil. In Matt. 10:33 to "deny" Christ is fatal to the relationship. In II Tim. 2:11–13 is an early hymn in which faith is affirmed in the faithfulness of Christ even in the face of our failing. It reads in part, "If we deny [presumably: him], he also will deny us; if we are unfaithful, he remains faithful, for he is not able to deny himself." Obviously, "deny" takes on different contextual usages.

To deny oneself, as embedded in the call to discipleship, is not simply to deny something to oneself. This is a popular interpretation, but it is false. Self-denial may involve the denial of something to oneself, but self-denial in Jesus' demand goes much deeper than that and is much more personal. To deny something to oneself is not distinctive to Christian discipleship. In fact, it is a widely followed principle, almost as wide as humanity. Few there are who are unwilling to give up something for the sake of some gain or advantage. The most egocentric or pagan people will deny various things to themselves in the interest of egocentric or pagan interest. A prizefighter will deny himself certain foods, pleasures, and convenience in order to win over his opponent. Most religious and political systems have adherents who gladly endure much privation and hardship in order to gain their goals, however selfish or inauthentic. It is no necessary test at all for truth or right or authentic human existence to be willing to give up something that one wants. The Epicurean denied himself many pleasures for greater pleasure. In modern times, few have matched Communists in their personal sacrifices for their cause.

In speaking of self-denial, Jesus did not mean simply giving up things one wants.

In the call Jesus gave, to deny oneself is to reject the idolatrous self who tries to be complete within himself. It is to say "no" to oneself, not just to pass up desired things. It is to reverse Adam's fateful choice, in which he said "no" to God and "yes" to himself. Self-denial is the decision to look beyond oneself in matters of trust, commitment, and love. To deny oneself is to reject the temptation to be egocentric, centered in oneself. It is to ground one's existence in relationship with God and his world. It is to reject the lonely "I" in favor of the "I-Thou." In the final analysis, this is self-affirmation, for the true "I" appears only in the "I-Thou" relationship and not in the isolated "I."

Closely related to the self-denial Jesus called for is the cross that one must take up. In fact, self-denial and the cross seem to be two ways of saying the same thing (Mark 8:34). The cross was an event at Golgotha where Jesus suffered and died by crucifixion. In this sense it was a single event, outwardly observed, belonging to a specific time and place. In another sense, the cross is a way, a kind of existence, belonging eternally to God and belonging necessarily to anyone who would enter into that kind of existence called eternal life.

That to deny oneself and to take up one's cross are two ways of saying the same thing follows from the elucidation following Mark 8:34. Jesus drew a sharp contrast between the attempt to "save" one's life (*psychē* can mean "life," "soul," or "self") and the willingness to "lose" his life for the gospel (Mark 8:35). The first attempt is inescapably counterproductive. The sure way to destroy oneself or lose one's life is to set out to save it. The self-centered life is doomed. It will self-destruct. The life turned in upon itself is cut off from that without which it cannot be authentic or find fulfillment.

This is the "Adamic" sin (Gen., ch. 3). It is the way of self-love, self-trust, self-assertion. It is also the way of self-destruction. In the Genesis story, Adam doubted God. He doubted the goodness of God, fearing that to trust him might lead to loss. Possibly God would withhold from him some good. So Adam turned to himself, to his own wisdom and resources. He made his own will final. He rejected any claim or authority above his own will. He made "what's good for me" the test of what is good. Meaning to save himself, he actually destroyed himself.

Egocentricity is the core of all evil. To nourish it is to open the way to all evil. To radically reject it is to cut the tap root to all evil. Why do men lie, deceive, steal, rape, kill? Men do this thinking that this is to their advantage. Men confuse good with evil. It is easier for man to tell right from wrong than to tell good from evil. Almost anyone would agree that it is wrong to lie, to cheat, to rape, or to kill. But at the same time, men must think it good, at least for them, else they would not do it. Thus confused, men often think the acknowledged wrong to be good and the acknowledged right to be bad. It is right to tell the truth, but it may get one into trouble, so men conclude that to tell the truth is bad. To lie is wrong but it may keep one out of trouble, so men conclude that to lie is good. But, trying thus to save themselves, men destroy themselves.

The cross is the reverse of Adam's sin. It stands for faith in God, faith in truth, faith in the right. The cross means looking beyond oneself to God and to other people. The cross is the rejection of the tight little circle of self-centeredness. It is faith and love without boundaries. It is not life closed and exclusive but life open and inclusive. Thus open, it is vulnerable to being misunderstood, resented, feared, opposed. The cross as one's way of life may lead to the event of Golgotha. It did for Jesus of Nazareth. It may lead to martyrdom, as it did for prophets of Israel and for Stephen. But although the cross is the risk of death and open to the actual experience of death, it is the only kind of existence that is really life. To "lose" one's life for God and for his gospel is to find life and to keep it forever.

Luke 9:23 adds "daily" to Mark's "Let him take up his cross" (Mark 8:34). Luke's "daily" is secondary, Mark's shorter form being original; but Luke's addition correctly interprets the intention of the logion. Taking up one's cross belongs essentially to all discipleship. It belongs to it at its beginning and throughout its course. Jeremias is probably correct in seeing that "taking up the cross" does not refer to martyrdom as such but to the lonely road walked by one condemned to death.[3] When one was sentenced to death, he took up the *patibulum* ("gibbet") and walked from the judgment hall into the street to face a howling, hostile mob. This feeling of rejection, of being alone, of being the helpless object of contempt and mockery, was worse than the death itself at the end of the way. To take up one's cross for the gospel is to tread a lonely road and to bear men's hatred.[4] For some, it leads to actual martyrdom. For every true disciple, the road is there to tread.

This principle of life through death comes to expression in various analogies and models in the New Testament. The grain of wheat must die to bear fruit (John 12:24). That it die is the inescapable condition for fruit-bearing. One must "hate" or lose his life to guard it; to "love" it is to destroy it (John 12:25). To be "baptized" into Christ requires that one be "baptized" into his death (Rom. 6:3). One cannot enter into Christ's way of life except by entering into his way of death (Rom. 5:10). Paul had already been "crucified with Christ," and he lived to tell it (Gal. 2:20). Clearly, by being "crucified" he did not mean physical martyrdom as such, else he would not have been writing about it. In Paul's usage, as in Jesus' call to discipleship, the "cross" is radical self-denial or self-renunciation in favor of committing oneself to God and his service, come what may. Only those who have "died with Christ" are among "the living" (Col. 2:20).

The radicality of the disease determines the radicality of the cure. Man's sin is not a skin rash. His disease is that of the heart. He needs more than salve for the skin; he needs open-heart surgery. In truth, he needs a new heart. Psalm 51 long ago probed to the depths of man's sinful condition and pointed to man's only hope: "Create in me a clean heart, O God, and put a new and right spirit within me" (Ps. 51:10). The psalmist prayed for "truth in the inward being" and for wisdom in his "secret heart" (Ps. 51:6). We have seen that this "new heart" with its Godly wisdom is one whose principle of life is the cross (cf. I Cor. 1:18–25). Paradoxically, self-affirmation comes only down the road which begins as self-denial.

LOVE THYSELF

Should one love himself? Should one hate himself? Should one do neither? Should one do both? There is no simple answer to these questions, not even from Scripture. As observed in other connections, words do not have meaning, only usage. It is true that certain meaning can be so associated with certain words that those words cannot be used neutrally, at least not in certain situations. "Fire," for example, is an audio symbol (spoken) or a visual symbol (written) with many uses but no inherent meaning. It can connote the flames from burning material, ardor of passion, trial, etc. But to shout "Fire!" in a crowded building is almost certainly to convey one meaning alone and is ruled a criminal act, unless the building is indeed "on fire." So with "love" and "hate" in Biblical usage. Neither word has meaning inherent in itself. There is no one-for-one relationship between either word and some specific meaning. Only the context can disclose what is intended in the use of these words.

Should one love himself? From Biblical perspective and in its explicit demands, the answer is both a resounding "yes" and a "no." Should one hate himself? Again, the answer is both "yes" and "no." Furthermore, one should neither love nor hate himself, and he should both love and hate himself. Is this confusion? Only to one who is insensitive to the chameleon-like nature of words, including the words "love" and "hate," even in their Biblical usage.

Hate Thyself. Jesus did teach that one is to "hate" himself. In stressing the cost of discipleship, he said:

> If anyone comes to me and does not hate (*ou misei*) his own father and mother and his wife and children and brothers and sisters, and even his own self (*psychēn*), he is not able to be my disciple. (Luke 14:26.)

This is strong language. It agrees with the logion in the Gospel of John, where to love oneself is to be self-destroyed and to hate oneself in this world is to secure oneself unto eternal life (John 12:25). It is yet more shocking when considered alongside another Johannine claim to the effect that to hate one's brother is to be in the darkness, to walk in the darkness, to know not where one is going, and to be blinded by the darkness (I John 2:9, 11). Furthermore, to hate one's brother is to be a "murderer" and to have not eternal life abiding within himself (I John 3:15). It also is shocking in the light of Jesus' rejection of the proposition that one is to hate his enemy (Matt. 5:43; cf. Lev. 19:18). What, then, did Jesus mean when he made "hating" oneself and one's nearest and dearest a *sine qua non* of discipleship?

"Hate" in the sense required by discipleship is obviously not the "hate" which is darkness, murder, and the lack of eternal life. Yet there is something which permits the use of the same term in such dissimilar ways. To "hate" in the sense belonging to discipleship is the radical "self-denial" which is linked with the "cross." To "hate" family and self is also for one to "bear his own cross" and "follow" Jesus (Luke 14:26 f.; John 12:24–26, 32 f.). It is a radical rejection of any egocentric motive and a radical acceptance of any personal privation, peril, or loss for the sake of giving oneself to God and to the service of others. It is the commitment to claims which confront us in the presence of God and other people, even if that means the loss of our nearest and dearest and even of our own rights or life. It is to pray, "Not my will, but thine, be done" (Matt. 6:10; Mark 3:35; Luke 22:42; John 4:34; 5:30; 6:38–40). It is the willingness to be accursed from Christ for the sake of one's brothers (Rom. 9:3). This "hate" is "love" in its ultimate expression.

"Hate" in the sense condemned as "darkness," "murder," and "death" (I John 2:9, 11; 3:15) is to hold another as without value, to despise, or even to ignore. To hate in this sense is antithetical to the nature of God and to authentic human existence. In this sense one is not to hate God, neighbor, enemy, or self. To find no value in oneself is wrong, the very same wrong as in finding no value in God, or neighbor, or enemy. Every man is created in the image of God and is precious to God. However marred and in need of redemption he may be, something of the image of God is in each man, in each neighbor, enemy, self. Each is precious to God and must be precious to us. Each is unique, unduplicated, irreplaceable. Each is an original, bearing within himself the autograph of God his creator and enjoying or awaiting the autograph of God his redeemer.

The only sense in which one is to "hate" himself is in the sense that Jesus "hated" himself when he risked the loss of all, even his family, friends, and his own life. Jesus himself gained his family only by first losing them. His mother and his brothers and sisters at one point seem to have so misunderstood him that they were virtually lost to him and he to them. This was the calculated risk Jesus took when he refused to yield to his own mother's notions about the person he was to be and the work he was to do: "O woman, what have you to do with me?" (John 2:4). Literally, Jesus asked, "What to me and to you, woman?" "What have we to do with one another?" It was not that Jesus lacked affection for his mother or that he was indifferent to their relationship. It was that there were commitments which lifted him above and pointed him beyond these ties with his nearest kin. His true family was the family of faith, the family of those who "do the will of God" (Mark 3:35). In this commitment he for a time lost his own mother, brothers, and sisters (Mark 3:31–34), and not until later did he gain them on a new basis and with new meaning. In thus "hating" his own kin, he loved them to the uttermost (John 13:1).

Love God, Neighbor, Self. The "great commandment" was central to the Old Testament (Deut. 6:4 f.; Josh. 22:5). Recognizing the oneness of God, it called upon man to love God with the fullness of his being. Pagan philosophy observed the principle of reason and order in the universe and concluded that behind it is an "unmoved mover." This was not the way the Hebrew people arrived at their monotheistic faith. Convinced that all men, with all their varieties and differences, come under the same moral-ethical judgment and care, they came to the faith that "God is one God." This faith rested not on scientific deduction but upon moral persuasion. With the oneness of God was joined the conviction of his love for all men and their obligation to love him with all their being.

Jesus validated this faith as the summation or embodiment of "the Law and the Prophets." He saw this as the hinge upon which all the Law depended. But he clarified, extended, and applied it. He not only interpreted it but incarnated it and called for the embodiment of love in us all. With our whole being we are to love God, but a second commandment is the corollary of the first. It belongs necessarily to the first. To love God implies that one is to love man, too. "Thou shalt love thy neighbor as thyself" (Mark 12:31).

Most overlooked in the second commandment is the requirement that one love himself. In Western culture we have been taught that self-love is wrong. Calvin called it a "noxious pest." [5] Freud saw self-love as narcissism,[6] the turning of the libido toward oneself. He held that when the libido is turned toward others it is love, when turned toward self it is self-love—thus making love for others and self-love antithetical.[7] Fromm demonstrates the logical fallacy in the notion that love for others and love for self are mutually exclusive, showing rather that it is selfishness and self-love that are opposites.[8] We properly love our neighbor as a human being, but we, too, are human beings. If it is proper to love another human being, it is proper to love myself as a human being. In those found capable of really loving others is found an attitude of love toward oneself. Fromm concludes:

> *The affirmation of one's own life, happiness, growth, freedom is rooted in one's capacity to love.* . . . If an individual is able to love productively, he loves himself too; if he can *only* love others, he cannot love at all.[9]

The selfish person is incapable of loving others precisely because he is unable to love himself.

The commandment "Thou shalt love thy neighbor as thyself" presupposes that one does and should love himself. One cannot love God and hate his brother (I John 2:9, 11; 3:15). One cannot love God or neighbor and not love himself. Either one loves God, neighbor, and self or he loves neither God, nor neighbor, nor self. There are two basic reasons for this: (1) the nature of love and (2) the nature of personhood.

The love commanded is a love which cannot be rationed, broken into parts, or limited. Either it is there or it is not. Love is the disposition to relate to another for that one's ultimate good, regardless of cost or consequence to oneself. It is not motivated by the goodness, beauty, or utility of the beloved. Eros is egocentric, seeking to acquire, possess, and use the object of its desire. It may be "heavenly" (*ouranios*) and desire the good and beautiful or it may be "earthly" (*pandēmos*) and seek the ugly and evil; but however directed, it is basically egocentric desire.[10] But the *agapē*[11] which God is (I John 4:8) is outgoing. This love loves us even when we are yet sinners (Rom. 5:8).

The love commanded is to be bestowed upon even the enemy who reviles and persecutes (Matt. 5:43–48). It is the love which belongs first to God and which we can have only by contagion, by catching it from him as in faith (the openness of trust) we come into his presence. This love is indiscriminate, bestowing itself upon the righteous and the unrighteous, the good and the bad. It can be commanded, for it is not just an emotion or sentiment; it is "not amiable feelings, but conduct patterned on the action of God himself" (Luke 6:35b; Matt. 5:45).[12] This love is "a matter of 'doing mercy,' which is to stop at no frontiers, leveling all barriers erected by national and even religious hostility" (cf. Luke 10:30–37).[13] If love is there at all, it is inclusive of all: God, neighbor, self, enemy.

For another reason, the love commanded is inclusive and not exclusive. It is because true personhood is inclusive. Repudiated by all disciplines now is the old anthropology which saw a person as closed and exclusive. Persons are seen now as open and inclusive. One's individuality is that which distinguishes him from all others, from God, neighbor, friend, and foe. But one's personhood is that which relates him to all others, to God, neighbor, friend, and even enemy.[14] Something of God is encountered in self and each other. Something of each other is encountered in

God and in self. To hate God is to hate oneself and all others, for something of each is in him. To hate others is to hate God and oneself. To hate oneself is to hate God and others. Conversely, to love God is to love self and others. To love self is to love God and others. To love others is to love God and self.

This principle of our relatedness is not a matter for Scriptural "prooftexting," although that is easily done. It is a presupposition deeply embedded in Scripture. It comes to explicit expression again and again. It is foundational in the judgment scene: "In that ye did it to one of the least of these my brethren ye did it to me" (Matt. 25:40). Likewise, to fail his own is to fail him (Matt. 25:45). Saul of Tarsus was persecuting Christians but was charged with thus persecuting Christ himself (Acts 9:4 f.). To divide the church is to divide Christ (I Cor. 1:13), and to sin against a weaker brother is to sin against Christ (I Cor. 8:12). The church is the body of Christ, not a body of Christians but Christ's own body. All suffer or all are honored together (I Cor. 12:26). God, neighbors, enemies, and we are so bound up together that to hate one is to hate all and to love one is to love all.

It follows, then, that it is not enough to love God and neighbor, or even to include one's enemies. The command goes farther: "Love thyself."

Selfhood Through Denial and Affirmation of Self

Near the end of his life Reinhold Niebuhr wrote a book centering upon the major theme of his life work, the nature of man in his individual and social existence; and he concluded the book with a depth analysis of the paradox of fulfillment through self-assertion and self-denial, entitling this chapter "Man's Selfhood in its Self-seeking and Self-giving." [15] He builds upon Jesus' aphorism "He who finds his life will lose it, and he who loses his life for my sake will find it" (Matt. 10:39). Niebuhr interprets this to mean that "consistent self-seeking is bound to be self-defeating; on the other hand, self-giving is bound to contribute ultimately to self-realization." [16] He rejects as misguided the disposition to denigrate or consider sinful all forms of self-regard and self-realization.[17]

Niebuhr warns against the self-defeating potential of self-negation, as when one attempts self-denial through self-will or discipline alone. This cannot be achieved simply through "a robust moral will." [18] Thus, to withdraw from the world in order to deny the self may involve one in "a vicious circle of preoccupation with the ego in an effort to get rid of it or suppress it," producing the pride which thinks of itself as humility.[19] He finds absolute self-negation impossible, "because the self is never in rational control of all the unconscious stirrings of selfhood"; and likewise absolute self-realization is found impossible, "because the self contracts rather than expands when consciously and consistently it seeks its own ends." [20]

The hope for authentic selfhood in its self-seeking and self-giving is found in grace (*charis*), grace as "the 'gift' of security, without which the self is incapable of becoming free of preoccupation with its own security so that it might relate itself to others and achieve true fulfillment of the self." [21] This is to see our hope to be in dynamics which enter into our personal existence from without, from God and other people, forces and factors which can redeem self-seeking from being counterproductive. It is to look to the "communities" (family, church, larger groups) which provide "the forces which draw the self from its undue self-concern." [22] Salvation is "by grace . . . through faith" (Eph. 2:8), and this saving grace includes "common grace," as in the security of parental affection, the crises which induce self-forgetfulness, and the causes greater than self which awaken us to responsibilities, loyalties, and the exercise of creative capacities.[23]

Into the frustrating enigmas of our personal and social existence God's love enters through the door of faith, through faith in Jesus Christ. It comes as free gift, grace. In the security of acceptance, we begin to turn from our self-seeking and to give ourselves to God and to other people, and in this self-giving begin to find our selfhood. As Tillich so beautifully put it (see Chapter 4), "One could say that the courage to be is the courage to accept oneself as accepted in spite of being unacceptable." [24] In the assurance of acceptance one is freed from the self-seeking which is self-destruction, freed to become and to be.

As seen earlier, although the cost of discipleship is the self-denial of the cross (Mark 8:34), our charter is abundant life (John 10:10). It is significant that the very religion which calls for radical "self-denial" promises fulfillment. The Christian calling begins with the call to "surrender," but it does not end in frustration or defeat. It is crowned with fulfillment as a human being.

The Apocalypse approaches its conclusion with the beautiful picture of the quenching of our thirst: "I am the Alpha and Omega, the beginning and the end. To every one who thirsts, I will give freely out of the spring of the water of life" (Rev. 21:6). The promise is sonship: "I shall be to him God, and he shall be to me a son" (Rev. 21:7). This filling or fulfilling cannot be imposed upon anyone, but it is offered to all: "The Spirit and the bride [God's people] say, Come! . . . And let the one who thirsts come; let the one who wishes take of the water of life freely" (Rev. 22:17).

NOTES

Introduction

1. Ernst Käsemann, *New Testament Questions of Today,* pp. 14, 116 f., is justified in challenging Bultmann's virtual equation of Pauline theology with anthropology, but even he gives it a highly important function in theology. Käsemann rightly sees early Christian anthropology as oriented toward the community rather than the individual, but it does look both ways.

2. H. Richard Niebuhr, *The Meaning of Revelation,* p. 31.

3. Quoted by Karl Barth, *Church Dogmatics,* Vol. I, Part I, *The Doctrine of the Word of God,* p. 1.

4. H. Richard Niebuhr, *The Meaning of Revelation,* pp. 153 f. Cf. also *ibid.,* pp. 8, 18–20, 22 f., 25 ff.; and *The Purpose of the Church and Its Ministry,* pp. 19–23, 31–36, 130–134.

5. John Baillie, *Our Knowledge of God,* p. 126. Cf. also *ibid.,* pp. 57, 157, 161, 174, and *passim;* and *The Sense of the Presence of God, passim.*

6. Wayne E. Oates, *Christ and Selfhood,* p. 36.

7. Cf. H. Richard Niebuhr, *The Meaning of Revelation,* pp. 7–22.

8. Quotations from the Old Testament are from the Revised Standard Version. Quotations from the New Testament are the author's translations or, in some cases, from the RSV.

9. I am not so naïve as to believe that one can unqualifiedly speak of "the" Biblical view of man, as though there were one clear, unambiguous view throughout. I do hold that there is a basic view of man that largely unites the Bible and that is sufficiently coherent to

warrant our using this expression without adding a cumbersome disclaimer each time it is used.

10. Cf. Abraham J. Heschel, *Who Is Man?* pp. 18–32.

Chapter 1. Created in the Image of God

1. Cf. S. H. Hooke, "Genesis," *Peake's Bible Commentary,* p. 179.

2. *Ibid.*

3. Gerhard von Rad, *Genesis,* p. 47.

4. *Ibid.,* p. 49.

5. *Ibid.* The concept of *creatio ex nihilo* seems obvious in Rom. 4:17, and there are wide traces of this interpretation of creation in Jewish tradition (cf. II Macc. 7:28; II Baruch 21:4; Philo, *De specialibus legibus IV,* 187, and *De opificio mundi,* 81). See Chapter 4 for both employment of this concept and reservation in its usage.

6. G. W. Anderson, "The Psalms," *Peake's Bible Commentary,* p. 414.

7. Cf. Baillie, *The Sense of the Presence of God,* pp. 35 f.

8. Cf. Martin Buber, *I and Thou.*

9. C. F. D. Moule, *Man and Nature in the New Testament,* pp. 2 f.

10. *Ibid.,* p. 4.

11. Von Rad, *op. cit.,* p. 57.

12. *Ibid.,* p. 56.

13. *Ibid.,* p. 58.

14. Leonard Verduin, *Somewhat Less than God,* p. 54.

15. Cf. G. B. Caird: "The Lake of fire stands at the end of the world's story as a proof of the dignity of man, whom God will never reduce to the status of a puppet by robbing him of his freedom of choice" (*A Commentary on the Revelation of St. John the Divine,* p. 297).

16. John Reumann, "Introduction," in Moule, *op. cit.,* pp. ix f.

17. I owe this insight into Job to my colleague, Professor John D. W. Watts, Louisville, Kentucky, and Serampore, India.

18. Ronald Gregor Smith, *The Whole Man,* p. 37.

19. Paul Tillich, "The Struggle Between Time and Space," in Tillich, *Theology of Culture,* pp. 30–39.

20. Moule, *op. cit.,* p. 3.

21. *Ibid.,* p. 4.

22. Cf. Wayne E. Oates, *Confessions of a Workaholic.*

23. "Evil eye" in Biblical usage denotes "stinginess" in the sense of "envy" (cf. Deut. 15:9; Prov. 23:6; Matt. 20:15). See Frank Stagg, "Matthew," *Broadman Bible Commentary*, Vol. VIII, p. 118; also O. J. F. Seitz, "Love Your Enemies," *New Testament Studies*, Vol. XVI, No. 1 (October, 1969), p. 43.

CHAPTER 2. ASPECTIVE YET HOLISTIC

1. Cf. Reinhold Niebuhr, *The Nature and Destiny of Man*, Vol. I, pp. 16 f., and *passim*.

2. Cf. Rudolf Bultmann, *Theology of the New Testament*, Vol. I, pp. 205 f.

3. David Stacey, *The Pauline View of Man*, p. 123.

4. The Hebrew of Deut. 6:5 reads *lev* ("heart"), *nephesh* ("soul"), *meodh* ("might"); the Septuagint reads *kardia* ("heart"), *psychē* ("soul"), *dunamis* ("power") (B [Codex Vaticanus] has *dianoia* ["mind"] for *lev*); Matt. 22:37 has *kardia, psychē, dianoia;* Mark 12:30 reads *kardia, psychē, dianoia, ischus* ("strength"); Mark 12:33 reads *kardia, sunesis* ("understanding"), *ischus;* and Luke 10:27 has *kardia, psychē, ischus, dianoia.*

5. W. G. Kümmel, *Man in the New Testament*, p. 43.

6. Cf. Ernst Käsemann, *Essays on New Testament Themes*, p. 129.

7. Bultmann, *Theology of the New Testament*, Vol. I, p. 194.

8. Käsemann, *Essays on New Testament Themes*, pp. 132 f.

9. Cf. John A. T. Robinson, *The Body*, pp. 8 f.

10. *Ibid.*, p. 50.

11. Cf. Oscar Cullmann, *Immortality of the Soul or Resurrection of the Dead?*

12. John A. T. Robinson, *op. cit.*, pp. 17 f., 31.

13. *Ibid.*, pp. 17 f.

14. Bultmann, *Theology of the New Testament*, Vol. I, p. 240.

15. W. F. Moulton and A. S. Geden, *A Concordance to the Greek Testament*, pp. 819–824.

16. Bultmann, *Theology of the New Testament*, Vol. I, p. 209.

17. Stacey, *op. cit.*, p. 59.

18. Martin P. Nilsson, *A History of Greek Religion*, p. 138.

19. Erwin Rohde, *Psyche*, p. 24.

20. Nilsson, *op. cit.*, p. 142.

21. *Ibid.*

22. Rohde, *op. cit.*, p. 6.

23. *Ibid.*, p. 5.

24. *Ibid.*, pp. 57, 253.

25. *Ibid.*, p. 257.

26. *Ibid.*, p. 265. Another view is that the idea of "soul" came from the experience of dreams, in which one seems to move freely from place to place and is even seen to converse with the dead, while the body remains immobile and at rest. Cf. C. N. Cofer and M. H. Appley, *Motivation: Theory and Research*, p. 20.

27. Cf. Stacey, *op. cit.*, pp. 62–64.

28. Rohde, *op. cit.*, pp. 374 f., 369 f., n. 42.

29. E. C. Rust, "The Greek Idea of Knowledge," p. 7.

30. Robert Leet Patterson, *Plato on Immortality*, p. 19.

31. *Ibid.*, p. 29.

32. Cf. I. M. Crombie, *An Examination of Plato's Doctrines*, Vol. I, pp. 296 f.

33. *Ibid.*, p. 297.

34. *Ibid.*, p. 303.

35. Summarized from Rust, "The Greek Idea of Knowledge," pp. 8–12.

36. The Gnostic saw man (some men) as composed of flesh, soul, and spirit—both flesh and soul belonging to the world and subject to the cosmic powers. But ultimately, man's origin was twofold, mundane and extramundane. Cf. Hans Jonas, *The Gnostic Religion*, p. 44.

37. Käsemann, *New Testament Questions of Today*, pp. 18–20, cautions against maintaining "a pre-Christian mythological gnosis."

38. Robert M. Grant, *Gnosticism and Early Christianity*, p. 6.

39. Robert M. Grant, "Gnosticism," *The Interpreter's Dictionary of the Bible.*

40. Grant, *Gnosticism and Early Christianity*, p. 8. Grant notes that Greek philosophy and religion might hold that a soul had fallen into a body because of its own sin, but the Gnostic point was that it was because of someone else's sin (*ibid.*, note 16).

41. Robert McL. Wilson, *Gnosis and the New Testament*, p. 9.

42. *Ibid.*, p. 143.

43. *Ibid.*, p. 6. Wilson here refers to Bultmann, *Theology of the New Testament*, Vol. I, p. 165.

44. Cf. Robert M. Grant, *Gnosticism: A Source Book of Heretical Writings from the Early Christian Period*, p. 16.

45. Robert McL. Wilson, *The Gnostic Problem,* p. 69.

46. *Ibid.*

47. *Ibid.,* p. 70.

48. Grant, *Gnosticism and Early Christianity,* p. 35, and *passim.* Grant sees the Gnostic to have changed the apocalyptist's temporal-ethical dualism to a physical (spatial–metaphysical) dualism. To the apocalyptist, Satan reigns over *this present evil age,* but God will triumph in *this world.* To the Gnostic, Satan is the god of *this world,* and it will remain under the power of Satan or hostile angels, escape beyond this world being the hope for salvation. Cf. *ibid.,* pp. 175 f.

49. Cf. *ibid.,* p. 184.

50. Cf. Wilson, *Gnosis and the New Testament,* pp. 4, 143.

51. Frank T. Severin, ed., *Humanistic Viewpoints in Psychology,* p. 133.

52. Stacey, *op. cit.,* p. 74.

53. Severin, *op. cit.,* pp. 133 f.

54. J. H. Randall, Jr., and J. Buchler, *Philosophy: An Introduction,* p. 213.

55. Severin, *op. cit.,* p. 134.

56. J. O. Wisdom, "A New Model for the Mind-Body Relationship," *British Journal for the Philosophy of Science* (1952), Vol. II, pp. 295–301, cited by Severin, *op. cit.,* p. 137.

57. Severin, *op. cit.,* p. 142.

58. Gerhardt von Bonin, "Brain and Mind," in S. Koch, ed., *Psychology: A Study of a Science,* Vol. IV (McGraw-Hill Book Co., Inc., 1962), abridged by Severin, *op. cit.,* pp. 151 f.

59. Eric C. Rust, *Science and Faith: Towards a Theological Understanding of Nature,* p. 207. My colleague Professor Rust is academically grounded in theology and science and offers a thorough study of "The Psychosomatic Nature of Man," *ibid.,* pp. 201–270, tracing the most significant theories and giving his own cogent analysis.

60. *Ibid.,* pp. 208 f.

61. *Ibid.,* p. 209.

62. *Ibid.*

63. *Ibid.*

64. *Ibid.,* p. 221.

65. *Ibid.*

66. *Ibid.,* p. 227.

67. *Ibid.,* p. 238.

68. *Ibid.*, p. 251.

69. *Ibid.*, p. 254.

CHAPTER 3. INDIVIDUAL YET CORPORATE

1. Heschel, *op. cit.*, pp. 44 f.

2. H. Wheeler Robinson, *The Christian Doctrine of Man,* pp. 30 f.

3. Nicolas Berdyaev, *The End of Our Time,* p. 80.

4. Baillie, *Our Knowledge of God,* pp. 42, 208–210, and *passim.*

5. *Ibid.*, pp. 209 f. The German epigram seems to be Baillie's own summation of Heidegger's position in *Sein und Zeit* (Halle: Max Niemeyer Verlag, 1927), pp. 117–125. Baillie's summation is a near approach to Heidegger's reference to "the phenomenological assertion that *Dasein ist wesenhaft Mitsein* (being is essentially being-with)" (p. 120). For the best English translation of Heidegger's book, see Martin Heidegger, *Being and Time,* tr. by John Macquarrie and Edward Robinson.

6. Martin Buber, *Ich und Du* (1923), p. 18. Quoted by Baillie, *Our Knowledge of God,* p. 208. For an English translation of Buber's book, see Martin Buber, *I and Thou,* tr. by Walter Kaufmann.

7. Friedrich Gogarten, *Glaube und Wirklichkeit* (1928), p. 57. Quoted by Baillie, *Our Knowledge of God,* p. 208.

8. H. Wheeler Robinson, *op. cit.*, p. 8.

9. Walther Eichrodt, *Man in the Old Testament,* p. 9.

10. H. Wheeler Robinson, *op. cit.*, p. 29.

11. Eduard Schweizer, *The Church as the Body of Christ,* p. 21.

12. Eichrodt, *op. cit.*, p. 10.

13. *Ibid.*

14. *Ibid.*, pp. 12 f.

15. Cf. *ibid.*, p. 13.

16. John A. T. Robinson, *op. cit.*, p. 58.

17. Wayne E. Oates, *The Religious Dimensions of Personality,* p. 284.

18. *Ibid.*, pp. 284 f.

19. Karl Barth, *The Epistle to the Romans,* p. 443.

20. Frank Stagg, *The Book of Acts,* p. 69.

Chapter 4. Made to Become

1. Cf. C. H. Dodd, *The Parables of the Kingdom,* p. 51, and *passim,* for the germinal idea.

2. Heschel, *op. cit.,* pp. 40 f.

3. *Ibid.,* pp. 41 f.

4. Oates, *The Religious Dimensions of Personality,* p. 53.

5. Käsemann, *Perspectives on Paul,* p. 5.

6. No one has pursued this more informatively or insightfully than Rudolf Bultmann in his Gifford Lectures, *The Presence of Eternity,* pp. 2, 44–46, 48, 140–143, 146, and *passim.*

7. Cf. Arnold Ehrhardt, *The Framework of the New Testament Stories,* pp. 200–234, for a careful review of the concept of *creatio ex nihilo* in Jewish and Christian thought. He demonstrates that both could work with the concept but that both sensed dangerous, pagan implications which were to be avoided.

8. The Greek *hōs onta* is probably not comparative but consecutive or result (*hōs onta = hōste einai*). Cf. Otfried Hofius, "Eine altjüdische Parallele zu Röm. iv. 17b," *New Testament Studies,* Vol. XVIII, No. 1 (Oct., 1971), p. 93.

9. Cf. Käsemann, *Perspectives on Paul,* p. 91.

10. Cf. Ehrhardt, *op. cit.,* pp. 200, 214, for Jewish and Christian retention of the formula that God "created the heaven and the earth, the sea and all that in them is" (Ex. 20:11; Neh. 9:6; Ps. 146:6; Jonah 1:9; Acts 4:24; 14:15; Rev. 10:6; 14:7) together with cautious employment of the more scientific language about creating the world out of nothing.

11. For these insights, see Tillich, *Theology of Culture,* pp. 120 f.

12. Cf. Roger L. Shinn, "Christianity and the New Humanism: Second Thoughts," *Review and Expositor,* Vol. LXVII, No. 3 (Summer, 1970), p. 318.

13. The essentialist points out that existence is the existence of something, else it would not be existence at all. As to the nature of essences, there is a wide range of difference among essentialists. They may fall into three classifications: (1) theological essentialism, which finds essences to exist in a supraterrestrial world or in God; (2) conceptualist essentialism, which finds essences only in the human mind; and (3) phenomenological essentialism, which derives everything from images or representations. For a full discussion of

these classifications, see Paul Foulquié, *Existentialism*, pp. 13–39. This whole discussion is heavily dependent upon Foulquié's excellent exposition of existentialism and essentialism, the most concise known to me.

14. Summarizing Foulquié, *op. cit.*, pp. 15–17.

15. *Ibid.*, p. 19.

16. Jean-Paul Sartre, *L'être et le néant*, p. 561, quoted by Foulquié, *op. cit.*, p. 92.

17. Marjorie Grene, *Dreadful Freedom: A Critique of Existentialism*, p. 139.

18. Cf. Käsemann, *Perspectives on Paul*, pp. 5, 13.

19. Cf. Baillie, *The Sense of the Presence of God*, *passim*.

20. Käsemann, *Perspectives on Paul*, p. 28.

21. *Ibid.*, p. 4.

22. *Ibid.*, p. 5. Also see Käsemann, *Essays on New Testament Themes*, p. 9.

23. Käsemann, *Perspectives on Paul*, p. 6.

24. Cf. A. M. Hunter, *The Gospel According to St. Paul*, Chs. 2–4.

25. Rudolf Bultmann, *The Gospel of John*, pp. 133–143.

26. Käsemann, *Perspectives on Paul*, p. 5.

27. *Ibid.*

28. Thomas A. Harris, *I'm OK—You're OK: A Practical Guide to Transactional Analysis*.

29. Paul Tillich, *The Courage to Be*, p. 156. Following a special lecture in New College, Edinburgh, spring, 1954, Professor Tillich remarked in my hearing that of all that he has said, he would most like to be remembered for this insight.

30. *Ibid.*, p. 157.

31. Tillich, *Theology of Culture*, pp. 146–157.

32. *Ibid.*, pp. 153 ff.

CHAPTER 5. FREE YET BOUND

1. Bultmann, *Theology of the New Testament*, Vol. I, p. 331.

2. Eichrodt, *op. cit.*, p. 9.

3. *Ibid.*, p. 17.

4. *Ibid.*

5. Cf. Heschel, *op. cit.*, p. 24.

6. L. Harold DeWolf, *The Enduring Message of the Bible,* pp. 93 f.

7. Eric C. Rust, *Science and Faith,* p. 218.

8. *Ibid.,* p. 207.

9. *Ibid.,* p. 209.

10. Ellis A. Fuller, M.D., "The Challenge of Biology to Traditional Theology," *Review and Expositor,* Vol. LXVII, No. 1 (Winter, 1970), pp. 34 f.

11. *Ibid.,* p. 39.

12. *Ibid.,* pp. 34, 38.

13. This blindness is not an arbitrary penalty imposed by an angry God; that theology is rejected by Jesus (John 9:1–3). It is "the wrath of God" as described in Rom. 1:18–32, the consequence of refusing what God offers. See Chapter 1.

14. Paul Tournier, *The Meaning of Persons,* p. 218.

15. Oates, *The Religious Dimensions of Personality,* pp. 198 f., 210.

16. *Ibid.,* pp. 210 f.

17. *Ibid.,* p. 212.

18. *Ibid.,* p. 214.

19. *Ibid.,* p. 290.

20. *Ibid.*

21. Trevor Ling, *The Significance of Satan,* p. 11.

22. *Ibid.,* p. 24. For a cogent study of the meaning of and distinction between "Satan" and "demons" in New Testament usage, see Ragnar Leivestad, *Christ the Conqueror.*

23. Käsemann, *Essays on New Testament Themes,* p. 39.

24. *Ibid.,* p. 40.

25. Hunter, *The Gospel According to St. Paul,* p. 75.

26. In Rom. 1:26 f. Paul employs the biological terms "males" (*arsenes*) and "females" (*thēleiai*) rather than the usual terms for men and women, presumably in order deliberately to picture man's reduction of himself to a sexual fragment. Even sex is further reduced to abnormal homosexuality, again a reduction from its intended fulfillment.

27. Cf. Frank Stagg, *New Testament Theology,* pp. 128 f.

CHAPTER 6. SAINTS YET SINNERS

1. Eichrodt, *op. cit.*, p. 27.

2. Karl Barth, *The Epistle to the Romans*, p. 347.

3. See Donald W. Riddle, *Paul, Man of Conflict*.

4. Barth, *The Epistle to the Romans*, p. 509.

5. The same Greek word or family of words (*hagios, hagiasmos, hagiosunē, hagiotēs, hagiazein*) stands behind the English "holy," "holiness," "saints," "sanctification," "consecration," etc. Cf. Stagg, *New Testament Theology*, pp. 104 f.

6. "Hagios," Gerhard Kittel, ed., *Theological Dictionary of the New Testament*, Vol. I, pp. 88–110.

7. Cf. Barth, *The Epistle to the Romans*, pp. 64, 68, 74, 84, 88 f., 93 f., 97, 100 f., 110, 186, and *passim*, for a compelling view of man's desperate plight in sin and his complete dependence upon God's saving grace.

8. See Stagg, *New Testament Theology*, pp. 95–102.

9. Käsemann, *Perspectives on Paul*, p. 82.

10. *Ibid.* Cf. also *Essays on New Testament Themes*, p. 75, where Käsemann finds that Paul makes "no basic distinction between justification and sanctification and did not understand justification in a merely declaratory sense."

11. Hans Conzelmann, *An Outline of the Theology of the New Testament*, pp. 219 f.

12. Käsemann, *Perspectives on Paul*, p. 82.

13. Walter Bauer, *A Greek-English Lexicon*, p. 197. For a careful study of *dikaiōsis*, see Stanley D. Clark, "*Dikaiōsis* in Romans," unpublished doctoral dissertation, New Orleans Baptist Theological Seminary, 1962.

14. Conzelmann, *op. cit.*, p. 220. Conzelmann is on target as he discusses "The Demand of God" in the Synoptic kerygma (pp. 115–127), as when he writes: "Moral effort does not bring a man into relationship with God; the relationship with God is given by God himself. Only then is the possibility for moral action opened up" (p. 122).

15. Bultmann, *Theology of the New Testament*, Vol. I, 253, 270, 276 f. and *passim*.

16. Cf. E. J. Goodspeed, "Some Greek Notes," *Journal of Biblical Literature*, Vol. LXXIII, No. 2 (June, 1954), pp. 86–91, for meaning

"made upright" as against the Reformation idea of "counting right."

17. J. P. Hyatt, "Habakkuk," *Peake's Bible Commentary*, p. 638.

18. Käsemann, *Perspectives on Paul*, p. 5.

19. Cf. Frank Stagg, "The Abused Aorist," *Journal of Biblical Literature*, Vol. XCI, No. 2 (June, 1972), pp. 222–231.

20. Cf. A. T. Robertson, *A Grammar of the Greek New Testament in the Light of Historical Research*, pp. 864–870.

21. So interpreted with reservations by C. H. Dodd, *The Johannine Epistles*, Moffatt New Testament Commentary, pp. 78 f.

22. On the whole question of the uncertain origin and diverse character of "gnosticism" see Wilson, *Gnosis and the New Testament*.

23. Cf. Fritz Kunkel, *Creation Continues*, p. 237.

24. John Knox, *Chapters in a Life of Paul*, p. 147.

25. I owe this insight to a former colleague, Professor R. E. Glaze.

Chapter 7. Salvation as Gift and Demand

1. Walther Schmithals in four books argues that Paul fought on a single front—against Jewish Christian gnosticism. His case is strongest as applied to the situation in Corinth, in his *Gnosticism in Corinth*. It is weakest as applied to Galatia, in his *Paul and the Gnostics*, where he finds the struggle against such gnosticism behind the letters to the Galatians, Philippians, Thessalonians, and Romans. Cf. also his *Paul and James* and his *The Office of Apostle in the Early Church*.

2. Cf. Stagg, introduction to "Matthew," *Broadman Bible Commentary*, Vol. VIII.

3. Cf. Reinhard Hummel, *Die Auseinandersetzung zwischen Kirche und Judentum im Mattäusevangelium*.

4. The antecedent of "this" (*touto*) is not likely to be "faith" (*pistis*), for *touto* is neuter whereas *pistis* is feminine. Although concord in gender is not invariable, it is a principle generally followed.

5. For alternate interpretations, see C. H. Dodd, *The Parables of the Kingdom*, pp. 176–180.

6. Joachim Jeremias, *New Testament Theology*, Vol. I, *The Proclamation of Jesus*, p. 98.

7. *Ibid.*

8. *Ibid.,* p. 112.
9. *Ibid.,* p. 118.

CHAPTER 8. SELF DENIED YET AFFIRMED

1. Oates, *Christ and Selfhood,* pp. 60–73, discusses "The Reconciliation of Self-surrender and Self-realization" in relation to the incarnation, culminating in the cross. Elsewhere, in *The Religious Dimensions of Personality,* he writes in this same vein: "The deeper desire of man for self-realization through self-sacrifice has only begun to be tapped by the psychological interpreters of human existence" (pp. 105 f.).

2. Roger L. Shinn, *Man: The New Humanism,* p. 95.

3. Jeremias, *op. cit.,* p. 242.

4. *Ibid.*

5. John Calvin, *Institutes of the Christian Religion,* Vol. I, p. 622.

6. In Greek mythology, Narcissus was a beautiful youth who fell in love with his own reflection, died, and was turned into a narcissus plant.

7. Cf. the analysis by Erich Fromm, *The Art of Loving,* pp. 48–53.

8. *Ibid.,* pp. 49, 51.

9. *Ibid.,* p. 50. Italics in original.

10. Cf. Plato, *Symposium,* 180 e *seq.*

11. This is not to say that a certain kind of "love" is inherent in the Greek *agapē* itself. In fact, this word can be used for hypocritical "love" (II Cor. 6:6): tax collectors can "love" those who love them (Matt. 5:46); and one can "love" darkness (John 3:19). But for the most part in the New Testament this word is used to express God's kind of love.

12. O. J. F. Seitz, "Love Your Enemies," *New Testament Studies,* Vol. XVI, No. 1 (October, 1969), p. 44.

13. *Ibid.,* p. 47.

14. See Chapter 3, on man as "Individual Yet Corporate."

15. Reinhold Niebuhr, *Man's Nature and His Communities,* pp. 106–125.

16. *Ibid.,* pp. 106 f.

17. *Ibid.,* p. 112.

18. *Ibid.,* p. 108.

19. *Ibid.,* p. 118.

20. *Ibid.*

21. *Ibid.*, pp. 107 f. In *The Nature and Destiny of Man,* Vol. I, Reinhold Niebuhr points out: "Man is insecure and involved in natural contingency; he seeks to overcome his insecurity by a will to power which overreaches the limits of his human creatureliness" (p. 178). Man then "pretends that he is not limited" (p. 179). He seeks to be God.

22. *Ibid.*, p. 125.

23. *Ibid.*, pp. 118 f.

24. Tillich, *The Courage to Be,* p. 156.

BIBLIOGRAPHY

Anderson, G. W., "The Psalms," *Peake's Bible Commentary*, 2d ed. Thomas Nelson & Sons, 1962.

Baillie, John, *Our Knowledge of God*. London: Oxford University Press, 1939.

———— *The Sense of the Presence of God*. Charles Scribner's Sons, 1962.

Barth, Karl, *The Epistle to the Romans*, tr. by E. C. Hoskyns from the 6th German ed. Oxford University Press, 1933.

———— *Church Dogmatics*, Vol. I, Part I, *The Doctrine of the Word of God*, tr. by G. T. Thompson. Charles Scribner's Sons, 1936.

Bauer, Walter, *A Greek-English Lexicon of the New Testament and Other Early Christian Literature*, tr. by W. F. Arndt and F. W. Gingrich from the 4th German ed. The University of Chicago Press, 1957.

Berdyaev, Nicolas, *The End of Our Time*, tr. by Donald Atwater. London: Sheed & Ward, Inc., 1933.

Buber, Martin, *I and Thou*, tr. by Walter Kaufmann. Charles Scribner's Sons, 1970.

Bultmann, Rudolf, *Theology of the New Testament*, Vol. I, tr. by Kendrick Grobel. Charles Scribner's Sons, 1951.

———— *The Presence of Eternity: History and Eschatology*. Harper & Brothers, 1957.

———— *The Gospel of John: A Commentary*, tr. by G. R. Beasley-Murray. The Westminster Press, 1971.

Caird, George B., *A Commentary on the Revelation of St. John the Divine*. Harper & Row, Publishers, Inc., 1966.

Calvin, John, *Institutes of the Christian Religion,* 6th ed., rev., 2 vols., tr. by J. Allen. Presbyterian Board of Christian Education, 1928.

Clark, Stanley D., *"Dikaiōsis* in Romans." Unpublished doctoral dissertation, New Orleans Baptist Theological Seminary, 1962.

Cofer, C. N., and Appley, M. H., *Motivation: Theory and Research.* John Wiley & Sons, Inc., 1964.

Conzelmann, Hans, *An Outline of the Theology of the New Testament,* tr. by John Bowden from the 2d German ed. Harper & Row, Publishers, Inc., 1969.

Crombie, Ian M., *An Examination of Plato's Doctrines,* Vol. I. The Humanities Press, Inc., 1962.

Cullmann, Oscar, *Immortality of the Soul or Resurrection of the Dead? The Witness of the New Testament.* The Macmillan Company, 1958.

Davies, W. D., *The Setting of the Sermon on the Mount.* Cambridge University Press, 1964.

DeWolf, L. Harold, *The Enduring Message of the Bible,* rev. ed. John Knox Press, 1965.

Dodd, C. H., *The Parables of the Kingdom,* rev. ed. London: Nisbet & Co. Ltd., 1936.

———— *The Johannine Epistles,* Moffatt New Testament Commentary. Harper & Brothers, 1946.

Ehrhardt, Arnold, *The Framework of the New Testament Stories.* Manchester University Press, 1964.

Eichrodt, Walther, *Man in the Old Testament,* Studies in Biblical Theology, No. 4, tr. by K. and R. Gregor Smith. Henry Regnery Co., 1951.

Foulquié, Paul, *Existentialism,* tr. by Kathleen Raine. London: Dennis Dobson, 1947.

Fromm, Erich, *The Art of Loving.* Harper & Row, Publishers, Inc., 1963.

Fuller, Ellis A., M.D., "The Challenge of Biology to Traditional Theology," *Review and Expositor,* Vol. LXVII, No. 1 (Winter, 1970).

Goodspeed, Edgar J., "Some Greek Notes," *Journal of Biblical Literature,* Vol. LXXIII, No. 2 (June, 1954).

Grant, Robert M., *Gnosticism and Early Christianity.* Columbia University Press, 1959.

────── *Gnosticism: A Source Book of Heretical Writings from the Early Christian Period.* Harper & Brothers, 1961.

────── "Gnosticism," *The Interpreter's Dictionary of the Bible.* Abingdon Press, 1962.

Grene, Marjorie, *Dreadful Freedom: A Critique of Existentialism.* The University of Chicago Press, 1948.

Harris, Thomas A., *I'm OK—You're OK: A Practical Guide to Transactional Analysis.* Harper & Row, Publishers, Inc., 1969.

Heidegger, Martin, *Being and Time,* tr. by John Macquarrie and Edward Robinson. Harper & Row, Publishers, Inc., 1962.

Heschel, Abraham J., *Who Is Man?* Stanford University Press, 1965.

Hofius, Otfried, "Eine altjüdische Parallele zu Röm. iv. 17b," *New Testament Studies,* Vol. XVIII, No. 1 (October, 1971).

Hooke, S. H., "Genesis," *Peake's Bible Commentary,* 2d ed. Thomas Nelson & Sons, 1962.

Hummel, Reinhard, *Die Auseinandersetzung zwischen Kirche und Judentum im Mattäusevangelium.* Munich: Chr. Kaiser Verlag, 1966.

Hunter, Archibald M., *The Gospel According to St. Paul.* The Westminster Press, 1966.

Hyatt, J. P., "Habakkuk," *Peake's Bible Commentary,* 2d ed. Thomas Nelson & Sons, 1962.

Jeremias, Joachim, *New Testament Theology,* Vol. I, *The Proclamation of Jesus,* tr. by John Bowden. Charles Scribner's Sons, 1971.

Jonas, Hans, *The Gnostic Religion: The Message of the Alien God and the Beginnings of Christianity,* 2d ed. Beacon Press, 1963.

Käsemann, Ernst, *Essays on New Testament Themes,* Studies in Biblical Theology, No. 41, tr. by W. J. Montague. London: SCM Press, Ltd., 1964.

────── *New Testament Questions of Today,* tr. by W. J. Montague. Fortress Press, 1969.

────── *Perspectives on Paul,* tr. by Margaret Kohl. Fortress Press, 1971.

Kittel, Gerhard, ed., *Theological Dictionary of the New Testament,* tr. and ed. by G. W. Bromiley, Vol. I. Wm. B. Eerdmans Publishing Company, 1964.

Knox, John, *Chapters in a Life of Paul.* Abingdon-Cokesbury Press, 1950.

Kümmel, Werner G., *Man in the New Testament,* tr. by J. J. Vincent. The Westminster Press, 1963.

Kunkel, Fritz, *Creation Continues: A Psychological Interpretation of the First Gospel.* Charles Scribner's Sons, 1947.

Leivestad, Ragnar, *Christ the Conqueror: Ideas of Conflict and Victory in the New Testament.* The Macmillan Company, 1954.

Ling, Trevor, *The Significance of Satan: New Testament Demonology and Its Contemporary Relevance.* London: S.P.C.K., 1961.

Moule, C. F. D., *Man and Nature in the New Testament.* Facet Books, Fortress Press, 1967.

Moulton, W. F., and Geden, A. S., *A Concodance to the Greek Testament,* 4th ed., rev. by H. K. Moulton. Edinburgh: T. & T. Clark, 1963.

Niebuhr, H. Richard, *The Meaning of Revelation.* The Macmillan Company, 1941.

———— *The Purpose of the Church and Its Ministry: Reflections on the Aims of Theological Education.* Harper & Brothers, 1956.

Niebuhr, Reinhold, *The Nature and Destiny of Man,* Vol. I. Charles Scribner's Sons, 1941.

———— *Man's Nature and His Communities: Essays on the Dynamics and Enigmas of Man's Personal and Social Existence.* Charles Scribner's Sons, 1965.

Nilsson, Martin P., *A History of Greek Religion,* tr. by F. J. Fielden, 2d ed. Oxford University Press, 1949.

Oates, Wayne E., *The Religious Dimensions of Personality.* Association Press, 1957.

———— *Christ and Selfhood.* Association Press, 1961.

———— *Confessions of a Workaholic: The Facts About Work Addiction.* The World Publishing Company, 1971.

Patterson, Robert Leet, *Plato on Immortality.* The Pennsylvania State University Press, 1965.

Rad, Gerhard von, *Genesis: A Commentary,* tr. by J. H. Marks, 2d rev. ed. London: SCM Press, Ltd., 1963.

Randall, John H., Jr., and Buchler, J., *Philosophy: An Introduction.* Barnes & Noble, Inc., 1942.

Riddle, Donald W., *Paul, Man of Conflict: A Modern Biographical Sketch.* Abingdon-Cokesbury Press, 1940.

Robertson, A. T., *A Grammar of the Greek New Testament in the Light of Historical Research,* 4th ed. George H. Doran Co., 1923.

Robinson, H. Wheeler, *The Christian Doctrine of Man,* 3d ed. Edinburgh: T. & T. Clark, 1926.

Robinson, James M., and Koester, Helmut, *Trajectories Through Early Christianity*. Fortress Press, 1971.

Robinson, John A. T., *The Body: A Study in Pauline Theology*, Studies in Biblical Theology, No. 5. Henry Regnery Co., 1952.

Rohde, Erwin, *Psyche: The Cult of Souls and Belief in Immortality Among the Greeks*, tr. by W. B. Hillis from the 8th German ed. Harcourt, Brace & Company, 1925.

Rust, Eric C., *Science and Faith: Towards a Theological Understanding of Nature*. Oxford University Press, 1967.

———— "The Greek Idea of Knowledge." Unpublished paper, The Southern Baptist Theological Seminary, Louisville, Kentucky.

Schmithals, Walther, *Gnosticism in Corinth: An Investigation of the Letters to the Corinthians*, tr. by John E. Steely. Abingdon Press, 1971.

———— *Paul and James*, Studies in Biblical Theology, No. 46, tr. by Dorothea M. Barton. London: SCM Press, Ltd., 1965.

———— *The Office of Apostle in the Early Church*, tr. by John E. Steely. Abingdon Press, 1969.

———— *Paul and the Gnostics*, tr. by John E. Steely. Abingdon Press, 1972.

Schweizer, Eduard, *The Church as the Body of Christ*. John Knox Press, 1964.

Seitz, O. J. F., "Love Your Enemies," *New Testament Studies*, Vol. XVI, No. 1 (October, 1969).

Severin, Frank T., ed., *Humanistic Viewpoints in Psychology: A Book of Readings*. McGraw-Hill Book Co., Inc., 1965.

Shinn, Roger L., *Man: The New Humanism*. The Westminster Press, 1968.

———— "Christianity and the New Humanism: Second Thoughts," *Review and Expositor*, Vol. LXVII, No. 3 (Summer, 1970).

Smith, Ronald Gregor, *The Whole Man: Studies in Christian Anthropology*. The Westminster Press, 1969.

Stacey, W. David, *The Pauline View of Man: In Relation to Its Judaic and Hellenistic Background*. London: Macmillan and Co., Ltd., 1956.

Stagg, Frank, *The Book of Acts: The Early Struggle for an Unhindered Gospel*. The Broadman Press, 1955.

———— *New Testament Theology*. The Broadman Press, 1962.

———— "Matthew," *Broadman Bible Commentary*, Vol. VIII. The Broadman Press, 1969.

———— "The Abused Aorist," *Journal of Biblical Literature,* Vol. XCI, No. 2 (June, 1972), pp. 222–231.

Tillich, Paul, *The Courage to Be.* London: Nisbet & Co., 1952.

———— *Theology of Culture,* ed. by R. C. Kimball. Oxford University Press, 1959.

Tournier, Paul, *The Meaning of Persons.* London: SCM Press, Ltd., 1957.

Verduin, Leonard, *Somewhat Less than God: The Biblical View of Man.* Wm. B. Eerdmans Publishing Company, 1970.

Wilson, Robert McL., *The Gnostic Problem: A Study of the Relations Between Hellenistic Judaism and the Gnostic Heresy.* London: A. R. Mowbray & Company, Ltd., 1958.

———— *Gnosis and the New Testament.* Fortress Press, 1968.

SCRIPTURE INDEX